CW00968851

A PROCU
COMPENDIUM

Articles from Spend Matters, Public Spend Forum
and more …

A PROCUREMENT COMPENDIUM

Advice, analysis and humour for buyers
(and those who sell to buyers)
everywhere

by

PETER SMITH

To Sue,

It's been a pleasure and privilege
to work with you all the years!

BROWN
DOG
BOOKS

Published under licence by
Brown Dog Books and The Self-Publishing Partnership,
7 Green Park Station, Bath BA1 1JB

www.selfpublishingpartnership.co.uk

ISBN printed book: 978-1-83952-045-7
ISBN e-book: 978-1-83952-046-4

Cover design by Kevin Rylands
Internal design by Tim Jollands

Printed and bound in the UK

This book is printed on FSC certified paper

CONTENTS

ACKNOWLEDGEMENTS

The originals of these articles – which I have in some cases edited, added to or otherwise adapted – appeared originally online, featured on various websites. Most were for various Spend Matters publications, including Spend Matters UK/Europe, Public Spend Matters Europe (which became Public Spend Forum Europe) and Spend Matters (US). A few featured in our Spend Matters UK/Europe newsletter or on the late lamented Search4Procurement 'jobs board' we ran for a while with a notable lack of success.

My thanks go to Jason Busch, my business partner in the European venture and Spend Matters' original founder, who first inspired me to try this whole 'procurement blogging' idea. His writing, insightful but laced with personality and even humour, showed there was a way of writing about procurement that wouldn't automatically send its audience to sleep!

More thanks to Nancy Clinton, our Publishing Director, who edited some of these articles and has been a great colleague and friend over recent years, and to Raj Sharma, the visionary founder of Public Spend Forum and now Govshop. And our readers, particularly those who commented on our material, and made sure I kept going through days when I struggled to find that really fascinating topic to cover!

I'm also grateful to everyone I've met in the procurement world who has helped me learn and understand more about our business, including those whose books have been useful and / or inspiring such as Dick Russill, Andrew Cox, Jonathan O'Brien, Sigi Osagie and many more – and practitioners who have similarly contributed directly. I'm not going to name them all for reasons of space, but most will know who they are if they happen to read this – thanks!

Finally, thanks to my wife Jane who got used to me seeing a chance for a procurement article in everything we saw, did or talked about. The price of cabbage – an article about global warming and vegetable crops! Choice of university for a friend's daughter – a debate about how 'open' the higher education market might be! A lovely skiing holiday – supply chain issues when your resort might be cut off by blizzards! You get the idea …

FOREWORD

I got into procurement by accident, like many of us in the industry. I still don't know how. I was working for Mars when the Head of HR tapped me on the shoulder – literally – and suggested I really might like to apply for a Purchasing Manager role. I was working in sales, in the office, rather than out on the road, with the plan being I would move into Marketing within a few months. I hadn't even thought about purchasing, but when HR suggested something at Mars, you tended to do it!

It turned out to be a great move, but I still don't know if Mars was just desperate to get me out of sales or whether the legendary Neil Coutts, then number 2 in the Purchasing Division, wanted me in his team – he knew me as we were both in the semi-serious Mars tennis-playing circle. So, either sporting nepotism / networking or incompetence at designing promotional material for the sales force explains how I got into procurement!

Writing was also an interest from a relatively early age. I wrote some sketches for Footlights at university, and after that dabbled with scripts for sitcoms, song lyrics, stories for my young daughter, and then co-wrote a proper procurement book, published in 2010.

I wrote for Supply Management magazine regularly, when I was working as a procurement director and then consultant, and then (as mentioned in the 'Acknowledgements') Jason Busch inspired me to start blogging to support my consulting business. That turned into Spend Matters UK/Europe and the rest is… well, if not exactly history, several million words of attempted wisdom about all things procurement.

This book is a collection of articles from the first few years of Spend Matters UK/Europe and associated online publications and newsletters. I've arranged it broadly by topic and included some short links and new explanations where appropriate.

Obviously, I have not chosen articles that related to very specific events or issues that were quickly forgotten, but where they were significant like the London 2012 Olympics you will find some references. Topics such as the latest news about tech firms date very quickly, I realised, whereas thoughts about good practice or economic analysis are often still relevant.

Anyway, while there is content here that has some sort of 'educational' purpose, this is designed to be dipped into rather than consumed at a single sitting. You might even decide to keep it on the bathroom windowsill, if you see what I mean - but most importantly, I hope you enjoy it, wherever you choose to consume it!

Chapter 1

BEING A
PROCUREMENT LEADER

Let's start this selection with some pieces relating to the whole business of being a senior procurement executive – what should you think about, who might inspire you, and so on.

I got to Procurement Director level relatively young, which was great in some ways, but looking back, I made many mistakes and perhaps lacked both experience and some external advice or guidance. So, whilst I would never presume to 'tell' people how to do their jobs, I like to think some of this material might be useful to people going through a similar experience to my own, perhaps coming to terms with a first senior role.

To start, an insight into my regrets relating to my time as a procurement director (for the Dun & Bradstreet Corporation, the Department of Social Security and the NatWest Group). I also commented about my successes, but I think the regrets are probably more interesting! I wrote a series of articles; here are a couple of those.

Things I Wish I'd Done When I Was a CPO

I wish I had fired more people

OK, let's start with a controversial point! Thank Guy Allen in part for this. At his Real World Sourcing workshop last year on 'the first 100 days of a new CPO' he suggested that firing someone was a good thing for a new leader to do in order to establish authority and 'pour encourager les autres', as he said.

My thinking is not quite that. It is more that I suspect I was too tolerant of poor performance at times. I've never enjoyed those disciplinary aspects of line management (not many of us do, let's be honest) but what I've realised is that you won't be forgiven by your peers and boss if procurement's performance is dragged down by poor performing staff. The image of your entire team can be very negatively affected by one or two people, and few of us have enough slack in the system that you can hide them away where they can't do any damage.

So, I wish I'd grasped the nettle on a couple of occasions and been more decisive. Of course, it is easier in some organisations than others, and it is notoriously difficult to lose people in the public sector, however badly they perform. Indeed, I still think that is one of the few areas in which the private sector is demonstrably 'better' than the public – in its approach to performance management.

Or you can just hope people go of their own volition – it does happen sometimes, and I can remember one occasion when I really gave thanks to one of our competitors for poaching a particular procurement manager! But if you really want to move the procurement function forward, your team is key, and you just can't afford to have people around who don't contribute. Be fair, be objective, but ultimately, be decisive.

I wish … I'd been bolder in terms of investment

It's never easy asking for money, and of course many of us in procurement are by nature fairly cautious with our money. One might even say a little parsimonious at times, miserly perhaps at the extreme? I don't think I fall into that category, but I was certainly cautious, and saw that as an admirable trait. Which in most cases and for most of the time, it is. However, there are times when one needs to be bold, and that was never something that came easily to me.

It's not impossible to drive change without spending money, but it is tough, it takes longer, and I suspect it is even harder to do it today than it was when I was a CPO. Investment, whether it is in tools and software, people through recruitment and training, or consulting and similar support, can definitely accelerate the change and increase the chances of success.

And what I've learnt is that generally the CPOs who drive the most visible change and the biggest success are prepared to put their hands up and say, 'I can deliver these benefits, but I am going to need some investment to achieve them.' I wasn't very good at doing that, partly because of this innate caution about spending money.

It's also worth noting that the best time to have the conversation is very early in your time with an organisation. Indeed, if you are really courageous, talk about it at final interview stage. If you don't get good signals back, then you can decide if you are still interested in a role where investment may not be on the table (it might still be a decent job but at least you know where you stand). If you leave it until you've been in the role for two years, the danger is the organisation perceives everything is fine, they like you, results look good – so why spend a million on a transformation programme?

The other opportunity where you may have to make the case for investment is if there is a 'burning platform' – or you can create the perception that there is one. But that's a topic for another day, I think.

Anyway, you have a choice. You don't have to be bold, and many CPOs do just fine without putting their heads above the parapet. But you only get one chance in life and one chance as a CPO of a particular organisation, so I feel I should have been a bit more daring!

I wish… I'd been more sociable with my senior peers and colleagues
Looking back, I think I was reasonably effective in the formal stakeholder management situations – giving a presentation to the Board or the like. But I could have been better in terms of that senior

stakeholder management if I'd cultivated my *relationships* with some key senior colleagues better. I'm particularly thinking about my time at NatWest and I'm talking about the CIO, the Group Property Director, CFOs and COOs for the major divisions of the bank – the people who were critical to the credibility, acceptance and indeed provenance of my procurement team.

What brought it home to me was when NatWest found itself in the takeover battle with RBS and the Bank of Scotland. In adversity, the senior managers got to see each other much more often, and I got far closer to people like the CIO than I had before, and actually ended up with a good relationship with him and most of the others. But why hadn't I got to that point earlier? A little natural reticence, maybe the fact that most of the people were a bit older than me and I hadn't been with the firm long … I don't know.

But certainly, one thing I could and should have done was the 'fancy a beer sometime?' tactic. Or coffee, lunch, whatever. Of course, we would have talked work, even if we had gone to the local pub. But just to get into a less formal situation might have helped in having some of those potentially challenging discussions about working together, roles and responsibilities, and so on. To chat about the tensions between IT and procurement, or how we could do a better job to support the retail bank change programme would have been useful to all parties.

Because however brilliant our category strategies or engagement roadmaps, relationships do still matter, and nowhere more so than in how we interact with our critical internal stakeholders.

***

As we're talking about leadership in this section, let's have a look at four of the many interviews I conducted. One was with a giant of the procurement world (John Paterson), one with more of an unsung hero (Paul Barker of HMV, a firm that was going through challenging times when we interviewed him, and the challenges have continued of course), Ellen Davis, a late entry into the procurement profession, and Jon Hughes, who never led a function, but as a thinker, trainer and mentor has been very influential in the profession. We'll start with him.

Jon Hughes

Jon Hughes announced his retirement as Chairman of Future Purchasing recently. After a career as one of the true thought leaders in procurement, including winning the CIPS Swinbank Medal a few years ago, I caught up with him for a very animated and fascinating phone call the other day.

So Jon, what are you most proud of in your 30 years plus in procurement?

Firstly, being involved in the 80s and 90s in defining rigorous processes for what we now see as the core of procurement – areas such as Category Management and SRM (supplier relationship management). That just hadn't been considered and systemised in the way that a number of us did then, working with firms like Reckitt & Coleman and SmithKline Beecham. And I still see some of our material being presented as original work by consulting firms and others even now – I can recognise our typos!

Then, I like to think I've contributed generally to the IP of the profession over the years with my writing, speaking and advisory work. I've always tried to get away from simplistic thinking and options and help people get under the surface and into deeper ideas.

What about regrets?

I've spent a huge amount of time helping to develop functional procurement improvement and excellence. I wish I'd done more in the executive development area. Why hasn't procurement been able to influence top management more strongly? When I have got into that level, it has usually been successful – even revelatory at times for the top team. But it doesn't happen enough, we need to shape their thinking more.

And on a similar note, I regret not doing more to develop procurement at MBA level. We have some universities offering procurement-related MBAs, but not the top ones, we still don't have LBS, Harvard, or INSEAD teaching procurement. The momentum seems to have gone on the business school side – we need to change the fundamental thinking of business leaders, help them get their minds around key business issues, understand how suppliers should align to the business. And the thinking in the public sector seems also to have regressed – where is the debate around integration of suppliers into programmes and achieving policy goals?

Which organisations have been the most stimulating to work with?

I've been lucky to work a lot in FMCG – Reckitt, Diageo, Nestlé – there's a real energy there and its always interesting working with the marketing community. Then there is Pharma – the link between procurement processes, suppliers and the whole research process is fascinating, whether it's been large firms like GSK and Novo Nordisk or smaller firms such as Lundbeck.

The third area is actually the public sector – the work I did with Professor Andrew Cox in health trusts was fascinating and innovative, we felt. The tensions in the sector between supply and demand, the complexity of the systems – there's still a need I perceive there, some big work needs to be done in health.

Which individuals have had a major impact on your thinking?

I was incredibly lucky to work with Ken Bowers, who was probably the first procurement consultant operating in the UK at the end of the 1970s. He was very much my mentor, and I dedicated my book, *Transform Your Supply Chain*, to him.

I've also been fortunate to work with some great, forward-thinking CPOs – Mark Ralf, John Dixon, Robin Cammish and others. I also have huge respect for Professors Lamming and Cox, even if I didn't always agree with everything they said! I've also met good people in the public sector – if I was continuing, I would want to put effort into that area. I think a few key individuals could still make a huge difference to public procurement.

***

Becoming a Procurement Person – Ellen Davis explains her move from HR

We're halfway through David Smith's year as CIPS President, amazingly, and we hope to get his perspective soon on how his Presidential theme is working out. You may remember he is promoting the idea of encouraging young – and not so young – people to join the procurement profession. That is both about explaining what a great career it offers, and also helping people get a foot on the ladder through apprenticeships and the like.

So, when a mutual friend told me about a lady who had made a very conscious mid-career choice to move into procurement – from Human Resources, no less – I thought it would be worth talking to her. What is her perspective on our profession, why did she take the decision, and how she was finding the brave new world of procurement?

Her name is Ellen Davis, and she leads the procurement function at the UK Hydrographic Office in Taunton, Somerset, in the South-West of England. The UKHO 'provides nautical charts and navigational services of the world's oceans and ports to support world shipping, including the Royal Navy'.

It's an organisation going through huge change, as its core business for the last 200 years, providing very high-quality navigational charts of the seas, is moving from a predominantly paper series of charts and products to a digital one, with changing production methods and new competitive challenges rapidly arising.

Davis was originally an HR manager in the MOD and moved to the UKHO 13 years ago. She worked on career development issues, and she says that she felt 'I should think about my own career in the same way that I was advising others to do!'

Then, in around 2008, she saw a piece written by Amyas Morse – he now heads up the National Audit Office but was then Commercial Director for the MOD. He explained that procurement in the MOD needed more 'managers not technicians' and outlined what a great career and profession one might have in MOD commercial. He must have been very persuasive, because Davis decided to make that move. She signed up for the MCIPS programme in 2009, paying for the first year of education herself, and before she actually had a job in the function – very brave!

Move on three years, and not only has she passed all her exams first time on her path to MCIPS, but she is also now Head of Procurement in UKHO. She now heads a transformed procurement team and has recently also taken ownership of delivering an on-demand digital print capability for her business.

'We're becoming less transactional – we've introduced category management, nearly all of the team are now CIPS-qualified, and we want to be seen as leaders in the public sector,' she explains. 'But I have found the public sector procurement constraints frustrating at times,' Davis says. 'We can't just "do deals" even where we see real opportunities; we have to stick with the processes.' (Welcome to the world of public procurement, Ellen!)

Moving from HR to Procurement seems a pretty unusual step?

'I do actually believe there are a lot of similarities between the functions. Take negotiation skills – they're certainly important in most HR roles. Supplier relationship management comes fairly naturally to me, I feel – like much of HR, it's about getting the best out of people, and communicating effectively.'

The whole area of managing internal stakeholders effectively is another where she feels there is a clear read-across between the roles.

'Persuading stakeholders of a particular course of action – one they might not initially feel comfortable with – is again something that both HR and procurement often need to do. I'd had some experience of the theory around persuasion techniques, but this was an area where the CIPS education was useful – we covered Yukl's 11 influencing tactics, and as well as the academic side of things, the opportunity to test the approaches in real-life situations has also been highly educational!'

(As an aside – it's good to hear praise for CIPS education, particularly in a behavioural rather than a technical area, which was historically perhaps the stronger suit for CIPS.)

Are there any areas where she feels her background is still a weakness or an issue?

'I've got very strong technical specialists in the team who understand the nuts and bolts of the MOD procurement process. I needed that, because obviously I haven't 'been there and done it' myself. I do regret that at times – I'd like to be able to get into the detail of the processes sometimes so I could contribute more to change and improvement. But I'm still hopeful I'll get there over time.'

Does she have any advice to others who may be thinking about coming into the procurement profession from other areas?

'Think about what you can bring to the function and the role. Work out what skills you have that will be relevant and can help to make procurement performance better. And play to those strengths.'

The links or similarities she sees between HR and procurement are very thought-provoking. Given the tension we sometimes see between the functions (often in turf wars over who leads on the procurement of HR spend categories), perhaps we could promote what we have in common as a means of establishing better relationships between the two professions? Anyway, many thanks to Davis, and we wish her and the Hydrographic Office continuing success.

***

John Paterson, IBM CPO, Talks Transformation

In this world where we tend to assume people move jobs and firms with some regularity, it is rare to find someone who has worked for one firm for over 40 years. John Paterson has done just that with IBM, including as their CPO since 2000 – an amazing achievement in these days of the two- to three-year tenure of many procurement leaders. So, it is not surprising that the Scotsman (albeit one who has lived and worked all over the world) is a bit of a legend in the procurement world.

And as well as presiding over IBM's internal procurement, with a third-party spend of some $50bn a year, he is responsible for the delivery of the procurement outsourcing activities that IBM carries out for dozens of clients globally.

We started by discussing the recent IBM CPO Survey. One of the interesting findings there is that firms rated as 'top performers' in procurement terms make on average significantly higher profit margins than the average firm in the sample. So, I asked him whether he believes there is a real causality there – does better procurement really lead to better profits?

'I think it is a causal link – I don't have any problem believing that. If you are spending millions of dollars with your supply base, how well you do this must have a positive or negative effect on the overall company performance. And we know if we can save $100 million through better procurement, that has the same effect on the bottom line as another $500 million or so revenue. And we are also delivering substantial cost savings for our outsourced procurement clients. If they didn't believe in it, they wouldn't pay the fees!'

Another finding is that CPOs see their priorities switching over the next three years from transactional systems, compliance and sourcing processes to supplier collaboration and more use of 'dashboards' with 360-degree visibility. Does that feel right to you?

'I think many firms are still in the phase where there is a short-term focus on getting the procurement foundations in place. In many firms, too much effort is still spent on transactional processes and efficiencies – so we need to free up some critical resources to interact and collaborate with suppliers. And the idea of the dashboard is a logical evolution. Better procurement organisations want stronger collaboration with suppliers and the days when the procurement role was to sit and wait for work have long disappeared.

The dashboard enables us to display what is happening and the value that is being added – it helps procurement and the organisation understand the capability that the supply chain can bring into our organisations. It gives us the ability to communicate better – for example the 360-degree view of the supplier, including their view of us.'

As well as the CPO report, you've published a short paper on procurement transformation. What do you see as the two or three most critical success factors for successful procurement transformation?

'Leadership commitment is vital. Living and breathing it, understanding and communicating why we are doing it. That means procurement leadership primarily, but if the rest of enterprise is against it, transformation won't happen. So wider executive support is also needed for success.

It needs a strong governance model – for instance, if we do a good deal and it doesn't get used because there is no governance or compliance, then we've wasted our time.

Thirdly, communication and collaboration with internal clients is key. You must show you are adding value and that they are being more successful by working with you. That builds and becomes sustainable as you can show success. And there are other points to consider of course – process standardisation, automation, people and skills, for instance.'

I am interested that you mention governance high on your list there. But in my experience, you can't force people into co-operating with procurement, a mandate is not enough?

'I agree, a strong governance model is not a basis or enough for long-term success – you can't terrorise stakeholders into using processes or contracts that don't work for them. But in the early stages of transformation – for the first year or two – it is important as it helps to get the momentum. Then you have to show the real value you are delivering.'

How do you keep transforming after 10 years or more – does transformation eventually come to an end?

'In the time we've been doing it, the overall IBM business has changed and transformed, on the basis of geography, products, focus, and so on. So, procurement has to keep transforming to meet the changing business needs. It is maybe not as fundamental as the change process 10 years ago, but it is no less important. And it gets harder to deliver increased value year after year. We need to get smarter and more creative every year.'

What sort of activities drive that value now?

'We are very proactive in looking at deep analysis of our data and seeking innovative ways of delivering incremental value. That may be commercial, or it could be demand management – we know better than anyone where money is being spent, what it is being spent on. We are also involved with strategic activities such as make / buy decisions, working on mergers, acquisitions and divestitures, both at strategic stage and post-event.'

***

Paul Barker – How Procurement is Making a Noise in HMV

How many procurement leaders these days started working for their current organisations while still at school as a 'Saturday boy' (or girl)? Not many I've come across.

But that is how Paul Barker started at HMV, the UK's leading chain of music / DVD / games stores, over 30 years ago. And *(at time of this interview)* he's still there, running the procurement function today, and still with a love of music and the performing arts – yes, yet another senior procurement person who still participates in live music!

After working his way up in retail to store manager, in 2007 he moved into the new corporate supply chain and procurement function, and now runs the small procurement team, managing the procurement of everything apart from what is sold in the stores – from marketing to store fittings – with an annual third-party spend of some £80 million. We came across him a while ago when we featured some promotional videos he had made that we rather liked, so he kindly agreed to talk to me.

One problem procurement can face in retail is that 'goods not for resale' is seen as the poor relation of merchandise buying. I asked him how he overcame that?

'That's certainly true to some extent. But actually, the financial pressures have probably helped our cause. Over the last year, we've positioned ourselves as people who can help the budget holders manage their budgets better and get more out of them. We've had a good response to that.' But he's also taken some positive steps rather than just relaying on the external drivers.

'I think when group procurement started, it was seen as a bit threatening by the budget holders. Perhaps we didn't explain clearly enough what we were all about. We now put a lot of effort into communication, and, although it's only a small team we're out and about a lot, meeting the key stakeholders.'

It's not just about communication, though. The team had had to demonstrate how they can add value.

'Marketing is a good example. There were some real doubts from the budget holders about our involvement. But once we got some solid external benchmarking information and were able to show the facts around some of our costs, we started making progress. We had to show the marketing colleagues and the suppliers we knew what we were talking about. In the end we were getting big savings, even in some cases existing suppliers making proposals to us to improve value, once they saw we were serious about what we were doing.'

So, what's his secret to successful stakeholder management?

'Be visible. For instance, we did a series of workshops for users to refocus our effort last year. We stressed that we were here to help, and we had the tools to do that. And communicate. I'm based in Solihull but I spend about three days a week in London because that's where many of our key stakeholders sit. Reinforce the basic message – we're not trying to take your budget away, we're here to help you make it go further.'

I wanted to come back to the videos and understand why he put the effort into that particular communication tool – was that part of the internal marketing strategy?

'Not really, to be honest – although when they got featured on Spend Matters, we got a bit of internal attention! It was really aimed more at the outside world. Given the difficult times HMV has been through, we wanted to show investors and the outside world generally that HMV was doing some good and innovative things to drive better performance.'

So, this was using procurement capability and performance almost as a 'corporate PR' tool – that's an innovative idea we don't see often. And it demonstrates an element of creativity in Barker's thinking, perhaps coming back to his artistic side, that made him a very interesting interviewee. Thanks to him for his time and good luck to HMV - I'll be back next week to stock up on new CDs, no doubt!

***

One of the longer articles here, but it is a great topic – what can we all learn from the works of Machiavelli? He really did provide some great advice, no less than 500 years ago …

Machiavelli for Procurement Professionals

Niccolò Machiavelli was one of the greatest political thinkers and philosophers ever. He's also arguably one of the most unfairly maligned writers in history, with 'Machiavellian' being used as a term of opprobrium to describe usually devious, evil behaviour. *The Prince* – his masterwork – is written in the form of what we might call today a self-help or business advice book, its topic being how to gain and (particularly) maintain power as a ruler in the complex world of Renaissance Italy, with its multiple principalities and republics.

I first read it many years ago and it was one of the few classics that far exceeded my expectations. I still dip into it, and I never fail to find it extraordinary that so much of his advice – given in a time when what we call Italy now was a mass of warring states, principalities, and religious institutions – is still really relevant to us in our personal lives and even more so in organisations of all types.

Coming back to his reputation, there is some basis for negativity, in that he wrote from the point of view that acquiring and keeping power was an end in itself. The end justifies the means, he says, in a manner that can be taken to be amoral. But if you look at *The Prince* as business advice, let's face it, not many of our contemporary works on 'how to succeed in business' are on a particularly high moral plane.

The Prince offers advice to politicians and rulers, particularly through the eyes of a 'new' prince or leader of a republic – rather than a hereditary ruler. So, as we get into what his work might tell us about being procurement executives, think of it as advice for a manager or director taking on a new role or joining a new organisation, or perhaps a post-merger or acquisition situation. Let's start with one of his best-known maxims – his explanation of why managing change is so difficult. And it is as relevant today as it was 500 years ago.

'It ought to be remembered that there is nothing more difficult to take in hand, more perilous to conduct, or more uncertain in its success, than to take the lead in the introduction of a new order of things. Because the innovator has for enemies all those who have done well under the old conditions, and lukewarm defenders in those who may do well under the new.'

So those who will lose from the change will make a lot of noise or worse, whilst those who will gain tend to keep quiet. But why are the winners so hesitant about supporting change?

'This coolness arises partly from fear of the opponents, who have the laws on their side, and partly from the incredulity of men, who do not readily believe in new things until they have had a long experience of them.'

People are suspicious, and don't believe that change will really happen, or that they will really benefit. Immediately, we can see why communication and persistence are two key characteristics of successful change managers. We must keep telling people what is going to happen and of course they must see that things actually are changing. Then those who benefit will support the change more strongly.

Machiavelli goes on to say that those who lead change – 'prophets', as he calls them – need to have real power as well. Now we can't use a few hundred guys with swords, which is probably what he had in mind, but it is a salutary point to consider. If we want things to change, we need to recognise it is difficult, and consider how are we going to back up our objectives. What power or authority do we have in our organisations? If our stakeholders don't want to adhere to our new 'no purchase order, no pay' policy, will the CEO support us?

Another of his well-known maxims is usually quoted as 'it is much safer to be feared than loved'. Indeed, this is often used to show what a wicked person he was. But the full quote is much subtler and takes us into some real lessons for management.

'One ought to be both feared and loved, but as it is difficult for the two to go together, it is much safer to be feared than loved, if one of the two has to be wanting.'

The perfect combination then is to be both feared *and* loved. But he acknowledges that this is a tough trick to pull off – although he does give some examples of successful rulers in the book who managed just that. As it is so difficult to achieve this combination, he suggests that, if you must choose, go for the fear.

And just to stress that his outlook was not wholly cynical or evil, he is also very clear that even if a Prince makes himself feared, he must act so that he 'at any rate avoids hatred'. We'll come back to that point later.

But expanding on the love and fear point – Machiavelli says that the ruler must 'proceed in a temperate manner with prudence and humanity, so that too much confidence may not make him incautious and too much distrust render him intolerable'.

So basically, he advises his theoretical Prince that his people should not be terrified of him (and indeed, as we say, he should aim to be loved), and that he should act in a reasonable manner whenever possible. However, the element of fear is necessary so that his subjects know that if they cross him, or rebel, they will be in big trouble.

Now we might redefine 'fear' in a less warlike environment

as 'respect'. And if we do that, isn't that what pretty much every business leader aspires to? We would all like to be 'loved' by our team (not too physically: I don't suppose they had sexual harassment issues in 15th-century Florence), but we also know that they need to understand the consequences if they are disloyal, don't perform, or let down the boss.

Thinking back to my experience, I've certainly had a few excellent managers where a sort of fear did play a part – even if it was the fear of letting them down, and of their disapproval, rather than a physically based terror.

And there is certainly a lesson for new managers here. Respect must be earned by behaviour, so by all means aim for love, but remember the importance of respect and fear. You must be prepared to exert some authority and power occasionally in a manner that demonstrates you are the boss. And you don't achieve respect just by being 'one of the boys / girls'.

That is also something Machiavelli covered. He talks about rulers who failed (usually they got assassinated) because they behaved in an undignified manner, indulging in sports and other pastimes (if you know what I mean) with the common people. That did not really gain them 'love' and certainly lost fear and respect.

In my time, I remember one new CPO in our industry who immediately recruited a bunch of their personal friends into the new procurement function and wanted to be both the big cheese and also 'mates' with the team. Their CPO-ship lasted about 18 months.

Staying on the leadership theme, one of the most controversial aspects of Machiavelli's thinking is his attitude to truth and laws. Basically, he is all for a ruler being merciful, honest and reasonable – until it benefits him to be otherwise! So, he recommends that his 'prince' should act consistency and within the law, and keep his promises, until it is necessary for him to do otherwise.

His stance in this respect is not necessarily immoral, but it is, we might argue, amoral at best. Yet we can still see how this works in practice today. Politicians value their image as honest people, but they don't hesitate to break election pledges when it seems that it will benefit them – or indeed the country. No university tuition fees? No more new taxes? Great promises until they no longer work politically.

And this is true of course in business. We might say to a supplier, 'We see our relationship as a long-term partnership,' but then move the business when a better offer comes along. Is that wrong? Well, it is not the highest standards of moral behaviour, but Machiavelli would argue that if it helps to retain power, then it is necessary.

In our context, if we behave morally and our firm goes out of business, is that an acceptable outcome? Machiavelli would say not, and would suggest that as situations change, so should our actions, even if we have previously indicated or even promised a different route.

Machiavelli also had a pretty cynical view of the general public. He suggested that the prince could get away with a lot – indeed, at one point he suggests it is easier to control the masses if they live in poverty. But he has strong views on how to be feared (which is good) whilst avoiding being hated (not good because you get assassinated)!

'Still, a prince should make himself feared in such a way that if he does not gain love, he at any rate avoids hatred; for fear and the absence of hatred may well go together and will be always attained by one who abstains from interfering with the property of his citizens and subjects or with their women.'

Basically, don't mess with your subject's property or their women is the message! (I apologise for the sexism, but this was 1500.) Now I hope not many Procurement Directors interfere with their subordinates' women (or men if we turn it around). But what about taking the 'property of his citizens'?

If we extend 'property' to include salaries, bonuses, company cars, pension entitlements, then we can see that yes, these are still amongst the most sensitive aspects for management. I remember the agonies of allocating the NatWest Procurement bonus pool, knowing that it was much easier to disappoint people than motivate them. So do bear in mind how sensitive these things are, and how easy it is to become hated as a boss if you don't get it right or are perceived to have 'stolen' what belongs to others.

***

Whilst we are talking Machiavelli and dubious leadership practices, the thorny issue of gifts and freebies came up occasionally.

Gifts and Hospitality – Recording It Doesn't Make It Right

I first came across the 'gifts and hospitality register' when I took a job in the civil service in 1995. Before that, I'd worked for Mars, where life was simple; just don't accept gifts or hospitality. Then Dun & Bradstreet which at the time was – let's just say, a bit more relaxed.

But the civil service had this register, it was explained to me. I should write down all gifts and hospitality offered (whether I accepted or not) by suppliers. Now, that didn't seem a bad idea – for instance, recording might enable us to see if a particular supplier had a pattern of making offers. What surprised me, though, was that some people seemed to see this as an alternative to a proper policy on gifts and hospitality. So, the two key points I tried to get across were these:

1. Merely writing it down does not make it right.
2. Getting approval *after* you've done something is not acceptable.

Taking the first – a bribe is still a bribe even if I write it down. Personally, I'm in favour of the 'no gifts other than advertising material of no resale value' policy. So, writing down 'bottle of whisky' does not make it any more acceptable.

Secondly, and this applies particularly to hospitality, I believe the policy should always include getting approval from the line manager in advance. Again, writing down '3 days in Monaco for the Grand Prix with Jim Bloggs, MD of our cleaning contractor' after you've returned to the office, Formula 1 merchandise in hand, does not make it right or acceptable!

The only benefit of a Register is that it does take away the additional element of secrecy which can take these issues into a whole new level of potential criminality, fraud or corruption. But in itself, the Register doesn't make everything right.

Why did this all come to mind recently? It was reports of Sir Paul Stephenson, Head of London's Met Police force, and his free-of-charge stay at Champneys, valued at £12,000. He apparently declared his stay in the Met gifts and hospitality register. But he seems to be saying that in itself makes it OK – which, I'm afraid, it doesn't, because we still have the question of whether it was *appropriate* for him to have accepted the gift of the free food and accommodation.

Now it doesn't appear to have been from a supplier or, thank goodness, from a criminal mastermind – it was provided by a personal friend, the MD at Champneys. But there is still a question of whether someone in his position should accept a gift of that value from anyone – even a mate. (And bear in mind that Stephenson earns over £250,000 a year.)

Might he feel in any way compromised if something came up to do with Champneys? Probably not, and he may well be a man of great honour, but how would it look if the police decided not to pursue something that had even some vague connection to Champneys or his friend? It's a tricky one, but it makes me feel uncomfortable (but I should say that my wife disagrees with me and sees no problem here).

However, coming back to our main point here – if your gifts and hospitality policy consists of simply 'record it in the Register', then that just ain't good enough.

***

And now one of the more unusual analogies I have drawn in my writing career!

Why CPOs Are Like Lady Gaga

As you will know if you follow my Twitter ravings, I've spent the weekend at Reading Festival, listening to (I estimate) approximately 60 bands. That does require jogging between stages (challenging in the mud) to catch 10 minutes of Band X before you run back for Band Y, which means you have to put up with drunk 17-year-old boys shouting, 'Run, Granddad, run!'

But - who cares …? And they tend to be pretty good kids generally, especially if you get talking to them and they discover you know a lot more about music than they do. You can also tell them stories about meeting Mick Jagger, Kurt Cobain, Joe Strummer and Madonna in a bar in 1979 and they'll believe you. It's all basically ancient history to them.

We have discussed the idea here that a key role of the CPO

these days is, as we defined it, to 'combine internal and external provision of services most effectively to maximise the contribution the procurement function can make to your organisation'.

So, here's a musical analogy. I've been reading Keith Richards' biography, and one of the interesting aspects is how tight the team was in the early days. It was the band and just a handful of people close to them. Now that changed over time as they got huge, but reading the book it is clear that, for many years, the key session musicians they used, for instance, became very close to the band and were very much part of the 'core team'.

A parallel in classical music might be leading orchestras where it is very much an employed team of people with a leader (conductor or musical director). There's some external input but it is the core team that is the key.

So, they are our parallels with the 'old' world of business and how being a CPO used to be, as in my day in the 90s where I managed 100 staff and used minimal external resources (people, technology, tools etc.).

Now, let's think about Lady Gaga, or any other big musical act, and how it works today.

Life is more complicated, and the stakes are higher in the global music business – just as they are for high-profile CPOs. But Gaga certainly does not employ everyone she works with. I'm sure a number of her most trusted people, whether musical, fashion, or personal assistant are employees of Gaga corporation. But not many, I would bet, and a lot of others aren't, even those that are key to her overall success – and that will include musicians, songwriters, dancers, technicians, publicists …

So her job is to lead the 'Gaga brand' (or the 'business unit' or 'function' as a business parallel, if you like), be the prime embodiment of the brand, take the lead on many outward-facing activities, and choose how she acquires and manages the resources (hundreds of people) she needs to provide the 'services' – the music and performances her client base demands and will pay for.

Blending internal and external provision, motivating both types to perform to the best of their abilities, understanding what they can deliver to the common cause – these are all skills that Gaga needs. And arguably she has done that brilliantly – and those managerial skills are pretty much as important as her own personal performing and writing genius. The CPO as Lady Gaga? Think about it.

***

Finally, for this section, a short but illuminating piece with some great advice I was given by a friend, who was one of the most effective procurement leaders I ever worked with.

What Makes a Top CPO?

I met the other week an individual who for some years has been one of the most respected procurement leaders in the UK. His particular skill from my observation is in managing his very senior stakeholders: peers and those above, up to and including the head of his organisation, with whom he has a very close and successful relationship.

After a certain amount of wine had been consumed, I asked him what advice he would give to others in terms of managing top-level stakeholders. I have to say this was a question of personal interest; looking back, I don't think I ever managed my bosses in as successful a manner as I would have liked. He identified three key areas. Two were not surprising, but the third was particularly interesting.

Firstly, he said, you must be seen as a *business problem-solver* by the C-suite. The old-fashioned purchasing / procurement approach of being a blocker, of putting process in the way of people getting things done, just does not work and will not gain you the credibility you need.

On the other hand, he said, you must not be afraid to say so when you believe something is wrong or cannot be done: *you must have courage.* (This is particularly important perhaps in a public sector context.) But, he said, you better be proved right! It's the crying wolf thing. In a public sector organisation, for instance, it is fine to tell the top team that something is simply illegal and breaks the procurement regulations. But if they get a second opinion from a top-tier lawyer, who says you're wrong, you're in trouble.

Finally, and this is what got me thinking, he stressed the balance between hands-on and hands-off work as a CPO. His normal style is very hands off, he delegates strongly and extensively to his team.

But, he said, if the chief executive is interested in a procurement project or contract, you as the CPO better keep very close to it. For these critical activities, the *CEO expects you to have your finger on the pulse*, to be able to answer questions confidently and quickly; not to have to say, 'I'll need to talk to my category manager about that and come back to you.'

So, in these key, high-profile areas, he stays very close to the front line, and is seen by the C-suite to be taking a personal interest and involvement in the issues that matter to them.

And I would add one further point. He has been in this role for about six years. You don't build trust overnight; you can make an impact in the first 100 days, but it takes years to build reputation.

Chapter 2

TECHNOLOGY

I've written many, many words about technology over the years, but most of them are not suitable for inclusion here, because the very nature of the topic means that commentary gets out of date quickly.

During my time running Spend Matters in Europe, my colleagues in the US were always way ahead of me on the detailed technology analysis anyway, but looking back, articles about particular companies in the procurement technology sector become irrelevant remarkably quickly, however insightful they were at the time.

Who remembers firms like Hubwoo, Iasta, b-pack, Spend Radar …? Names that used to mean a lot and would be regularly featured by Spend Matters and others. But the pace of acquisitions and mergers has been considerable, and those firms and many more got swallowed up. Equally, anything about specific technology innovations becomes old news pretty quickly. Articles explaining the benefits of this new 'cloud' idea look very ancient now!

But in putting this collection together, it was fun to look back at articles about an interesting 'small' firm called Coupa, who within a few years of course became one of the 600-pound tech gorillas of our sector. But for every success, there is a failure, like IBM's ill-fated acquisition of Emptoris (remember them?) And some of my writing did address issues that have continuing resonance – such as how your supply base might feel about new technology, or the trade-offs between functionality and ease of use in terms of procurement software.

But we'll start with a personal story about my own life with technology. Just think, if my university had taught me a programming language that wasn't ONLY used in the Cambridge Maths Department, I might have been the British Bill Gates…

The Good Old Days: Allegros and Procurement Software

I learnt to programme on the Cambridge University Maths Department mainframe computer in 1977. It had the distinction of having a totally unique programming language, used on not one other computer in the entire world.

The Department was quite proud of this (which says something about the attitude of the Maths Department, which I remember with an almost total lack of fondness). I, on the other hand, couldn't help thinking that this made the hours sitting there somewhat wasted; time that could have been better spent on the football field, in the bar – or pretty much anywhere, to be honest. Even learning something useful.

Then, after graduating, one of my early jobs at Mars Confectionery was writing a new computerised factory costing system, which was more fun, as I could stay late and play a very early version of a computer game – mainframe-based, green screen and totally text-based.

'What do you want to do?'

I would type 'Shoot the two-headed bull with the crossbow'… (then wait five minutes)…

'You have missed and been eaten by the giant orc. Go back to step 3.'

It wasn't exactly *Line of Duty 3*.

But, despite this early exposure, I didn't sustain any deep interest in technology, although I was always interested in what it could do for me as a manager. But, a few years later, I got deeply suspicious of the ERP business case I was asked to sign as the CPO of large organisations where the entire investment (HR, Finance, Procurement) was to be justified by '3% savings on £1 billion procurement spend'.

How exactly was that going to happen then? And couldn't we achieve that with better governance and a few more skilled procurement folk – for a fraction of the cost? And why did the system we were buying want me to express complex services we purchased in 'units' with a 'cost per unit', a 'delivery date' and a 'stock level', when that clearly made no sense at all?

Anyway, since I've been blogging, one thing has struck me probably above all else; and that is how quickly technology aimed at our profession has improved in the last 10 years or so. Cars provide a good analogy. I remember when some cars were really, really bad. Choosing a model was fraught with danger, particularly if it hadn't been on the market for long. Would it turn out to be another Austin Allegro – or the Fiat my father bought in the late-1960s, of which my only memory is sitting in it, motionless in the driveway, with my father under the bonnet. I have no memory of actually travelling anywhere in it, although I suppose it must have moved occasionally …

But now, there is hardly a 'bad' car on the market. Sure, some are better than others, but nothing compares to the disasters of the 60s and 70s.

And it strikes me that technology – and I'm thinking software particularly here – is much the same. Anything that gets to market and is seriously promoted is almost certainly pretty good. For most procurement-related needs, there is a good choice of products; that doesn't mean you don't need to select carefully, understanding your needs clearly and looking for what best meets them. And of course, there are a wide range of commercial models, level of services provided alongside, and so on. But your chances of buying something that is fundamentally rubbish is these days thankfully low.

So, when people complain that everything is worse than it used to be, remind them of the Austin Allegro, little Jimmy Osmond, and text-based dungeons and dragons!

***

So, when I first came across SAP, I had no idea the firm would become the massively successful giant it is today…

Build Your Own P2P System (If You're Crazy)

Checking their website, it tells me that SAP opened their first office in the UK in 1987. And I believe I visited it that year – Aylesbury or somewhere like that? At Mars Confectionery we had decided that we should have a 'purchasing computer system' so I went to talk to SAP along with a lady from the Mars internal computer services division. (She played on the wing for the England Ladies Rugby Team, and there will be more about her in my autobiography, 'Interesting People I Have Known', to be published in 2038…)

Anyway, moving on, Mars decided to develop their own system – might that have been partly because the computer services division saw it as a good revenue-earning project? I couldn't possibly comment. But I left not long after that, and I have a suspicion that by the time it was built and implemented some years later, the technology world had moved on considerably, and I'd guess building our own system probably didn't look like the smartest move in retrospect.

Of course, no one would build their own purchase-to-pay system now, would they? Not with all the options available on the market, the maturity and capability that's available off the shelf, and the relatively lower cost than we would have paid all those years ago. But wait!

I have it on good authority that a very, very large global company (global top 100) is looking to 'build their own' – with the help of one of the global giant IT / consulting firms, of course. That seems astonishing, to be honest – but let's try and think objectively about the pros and cons of such a move.

Issues with build your own
- Very large and possibly open-ended cost
- Dependent on the ability of the IT firm
- Long lead times with little guarantee of hitting any initially quoted timescales
- High-risk – a solution that is by definition untried, unproven
- No automatic upgrade path (with costs defrayed across multiple users) – further costs inevitable and unending
- No available pool of expertise – technology or procurement – familiar with the system
- Potential integration issues with other technology

Positives
- Ability to specify – and hopefully get – just what you want to meet your needs
- A major project that will occupy lots of time and people within the firm for years (good for the people, not necessarily the firm)

And for positives, that's all I could come up with. You can probably tell which side of the argument I'm coming down on. It seems like a surprising strategy, to say the least – but we're very open to any further thoughts or explanation as to why this would be the right way to go.

Or is this another example of what we call 'Stupid Sourcing'? And this time, that stupidity comes from a procurement function itself, rather than a misguided bunch of non-procurement stakeholders!

***

Here is a nice example of an innovative use of e-sourcing technology from Nick Drewe, a founder of software firm Market Dojo. We asked Nick recently (2019) what the outcome had been from this, and he told us, "The end result was a £35,000 saving versus the four original quotes sourced by our architect. We actually selected the 2nd most competitive supplier, as their attention to detail was superior. The job was completed on time and only a few percent over budget, despite upgrades to certain specifications. The 'contract management' aspect of the relationship was smooth, owing to the thoroughness of the tender. In fact, the supplier was consequently referred by us to five other clients, who were equally impressed. It's satisfying that our promise of referrals in return for a competitive offer has been fulfilled, to create a true win-win-win!"

e-Sourcing Comes to the Home

Well done to Nick Drewe of Market Dojo, sourcing solutions providers. He is following his own advice and running an e-sourcing (and possibly auction) process to choose a builder to carry out some fairly major works on his home in Bristol in the West of England. He's writing about it on the Market Dojo website and LinkedIn, and we've had a couple of instalments so far. Here is an extract.

'Ben drew up a very comprehensive tender package, including all drawings, national standards, specifications, and a detailed list of the scope of works, and has approached four contractors that he has worked with in the past. Two of those contractors haven't even bothered quoting for the job. The other two came in with quotes of £93,000 and £98,000, both excluding VAT. The quotes have been paper-based and are barely comparable, with wildly different items included within their cost breakdown. Therefore, not only are they greatly over budget, but I also have no confidence that they even fulfil the requirement.

And so I've decided to take things into my own hands. I shall distribute the tender package (all 20 megabytes of it) to the Bristol building trade as a whole to find out a) what the real market price is for my extension works; and b) to make sure they quote and deliver exactly what we've asked for.'

In his part 2 he describes how he found over 80 builders to contact in the first place, but we're now waiting to see how many will actually participate in the event. Several have downloaded documents and drawings from the sourcing portal ... we're awaiting part 3 with interest!

Not only might this prove to be a success for his project, as well as being a fun topic to cover, it also does throw up some deeper questions. Can auctions be used for pretty much anything? And perhaps most striking is the thought that there might be domestic applications for some B2B e-sourcing tools. Might a consumer be able to use sourcing tools when buying a new car? A holiday?

I suppose in a sense we already do use tools that read across to corporate solutions – I've recently browsed online catalogues, checked ratings websites and feedback before booking next year's skiing holiday. But we didn't run a sourcing event to see which hotels or tour firms might offer us a better deal – or indeed use market-informed sourcing to determine whether we should book the different elements of the holiday separately or bundle it with a travel agent!

One barrier is that you need to have some real competition to get the benefit of tools and indeed of the processes themselves. So, it is less applicable if you definitely know which hotel in Obertauern you want to visit, as in our case.

Another issue for the consumer is that we often don't have significant *repeat business to offer*, unlike most corporate situations. So, if Nick accepts a low bid, will the builder really care about doing a great job, knowing that he probably isn't going to buy another project for some time, if ever? Although in this case I suppose if the firm knows this is pretty high-profile in the procurement world, at least that might be a decent incentive for them to perform!

***

Sometimes my thinking got quite science-fiction…

Keeping up with the kids – a challenge for technology providers

I loved this opening to an article in *The Times* (behind their paywall unfortunately) from Bridget Harrison about how young children are becoming tech-savvy at an incredibly early age.

'My early rising five-year-old cannot yet tell the time, so the other day I left my iPhone by his bed with strict instructions not to wake us up until it said 7.00. I turned it to Airplane mode, which shuts down the phone and wi-fi, just in case he accidentally called America.

Next day he appeared at my bedside at seven on the dot having had a high old time. He'd gone into Settings, turned off Airplane mode, takes some pictures of his teddies and texted them to his favourite auntie. Then he'd changed the wallpaper on my home screen to a picture of him in his school uniform. He'd gone into Voice Notes (which I had yet to discover) and recorded himself making raaring noises, and he'd reset my ring tone to *Choo Choo*.'

That got me thinking about the challenges faced by software firms, including in our field. They're all looking to make their products more user-friendly, aiming for more of a consumer-type experience than the traditional and often painful B2B, old-style

ERP experience. Every P2P company now talks about Amazon or eBay as the model for their interfaces, and for firms such as Coupa, it is at the heart of their success.

But arguably the user is still moving faster than the firms can respond. If this five-year-old is already a sophisticated technology user, where will we be in five or 10 years' time? We're in the midst of a huge boom in mobile right now, which solution providers are desperately trying to keep up with, but what will be next?

Will today's five-year-olds expect everything to be voice-controlled by the time they're thinking of joining the workforce of the late 2020s? Or will it be motion-driven controls, or systems that track our eye movements? (Hang on, that's already here.) Will stand-alone mobile devices be old hat because all the capability will be contained within wearable technology?

Will we wear our special glasses or maybe even contact lenses with projection of what we currently get on-screen in front of our eyes, or perhaps we'll just have a chip implanted at birth so we will be able to raise or approve a requisition by the power of thought alone?

Will artificial intelligence take away the need for much human thought at all, in the way that Google has destroyed the need for us to remember anything?

By then, I suspect personally I won't be worrying too much about the impact of technological change on procurement processes and technology. I'll be in my full-immersion 3-D alternative reality pod, playing bass guitar as my virtual and wholly imaginary band headlines a huge rock festival. And as for the after-show parties… Sorry, Angelina, Rachel, Emma, bit tired tonight, think I had too much of that Latour '61 again.

Joking aside, the pace of change in terms of consumer expectation and capability is a huge challenge and yet an opportunity for software firms and those in related industries. It is likely to lead to market volatility on the provider side, with the potential for firms to grow and perhaps shrink rapidly.

All very exciting, if a bit scary. But anyway, see you at our virtual gig, Glastonbury, 2028…

***

I first met Rob Bernshteyn in (I think) early 2010, when a friend of mine roped me in to a small gathering in the Institute of Directors to meet him on his first trip to the UK since he had become CEO of Coupa. No one had heard of the firm, and there were literally just a handful of random procurement and tech folk there for a few drinks and chat. Scroll on a few years, and Coupa is now valued at some $2 billion. Here are a couple of pieces relating to their journey. Do you remember when 'the Cloud' was new and sexy?

Introducing Coupa

We mentioned Coupa in the context of their tie-up with Emptoris, but they weren't an organisation I knew much about, so I caught up with Ashish Deshpande of the firm the other day for an introductory briefing.

They operate in the purchase-to-pay, transactional management space, covering both procurement and expense management (travel etc.) 'Cloud-based spend management' is the proposition. They've been going since 2006, the founders being veterans from software firms including Oracle.

At the moment their customer base is largely US firms, which takes them into Europe via the subsidiaries of those clients, but they are looking to develop more presence this side of the Atlantic. Tesco

Bank is an early UK-based client; Salesforce.com is an example of a US-based client with major EMEA operations as well.

They work with partners (often consulting firms) in various countries who provide a sales channel – for instance, Procurra in the UK. Serious moves into Europe are coming 'later this year' with multi-language product versions being launched.

The product itself offers a platform with four elements; 'smarter procurement', expense management, an 'executive dashboard' and 'real-time benchmarking'. It provides a single interface at the point of demand; so it gives the client a single solution for controlling all non-payroll spend 'in the cloud'. The proposition is around ease of use for the end-user, which Coupa believe (and I agree) drives better compliance and adoption. As Jason Busch said last March:

> Coupa excels in the overall user, administrator and management experience. At all levels, Coupa has really thought through the essential information a user needs to consume with a minimum amount of navigational fuss.

For instance, approvals (of requisitions, for example) can be carried out via mobile devices, making it more likely that managers will do what they're supposed to in a timely manner.

There are some innovative features as well: the technology can automatically 'score' expense management claims against the organisation's expense policy, then report with suggestions as to which claims need to be manually inspected. And the benchmarking facility is interesting, allowing the user to compare their own performance with other Coupa users (not in terms of prices, but in areas such as cycle time and process efficiency).

Coupa connects with ERP systems and in effect sits on top of them, offering a more user-friendly approach to controlling the P2P process. And Deshpande had an interesting take on this: ERP systems are, as he put it, 'the system of record'. They probably need to sit within the organisation's ownership and firewall, as it were. But cloud-based platforms like Coupa can be more flexible and offer much more flexible and user-friendly options in terms of transactional management.

They're up against tough competition; Ariba obviously, but also serious European players such as Basware, Proactis, Hubwoo and others. But Coupa's growth in the US has been impressive, and they've got a reputation for feisty, assertive marketing, as seen when they took on Ariba directly in a marketing campaign! So once they are fully active in Europe, they will be an interesting option to consider in this space.

***

Advice to Buyers of Procurement Technology

One of our meetings when Jason Busch (Spend Matters founder) was here last week was with Coupa. We know Alex Kleiner well, now the regional EMEA Vice-President, but he also introduced two of his rapidly expanding team – Andy Lightfoot, Sales Director for EMEA and Ronan Kerouedan, Director, Solutions Consulting for EMEA also.

The speed of expansion and recruitment is impressive, and Coupa's European wins are into double figures, with some very large deals at final stages (sometimes with competitors still in the frame, we should point out). They're also developing their 'channels', with links to large systems integrators and consulting firms as well.

The team are finding that generally firms in Europe take longer to make decisions than their US counterparts – more caution and a wider circle of internal stakeholders to involve perhaps, with collaborative approaches to decision-making the norm. The economic situation may play into this as well, given Europe's continued struggles, although effective procurement software should have a great ROI for most organisations. But we expect to see some impressive customer wins from Coupa through the rest of this year as they offer serious competition to both the ERP-type giants and local European players.

And one positive development for the procurement technology industry generally is that 'cloud' is bringing advanced technology within reach of mid-market firms for the first time, from the point of view of both cost and ease of implementation and management of the system.

That is reflected in Coupa finding that over 50% of their prospects are 'greenfield sites', in the sense that they don't have any current P2P-installed platform. But rather than just the Coupa update, we thought it would be interesting to pick the brains of the three Coupa experts. So, we asked them a question.

'Given you're in the middle of quite a few major tender processes, where CPOs or equivalent are investing in purchase-to-pay (and sometimes more), what three bits of advice would you give to anyone on the buy side in a similar position?' That certainly stimulated a lively debate, and eventually we arrived at these three points.

1. Get your colleagues who are key stakeholders involved reasonably early in the process. 'If the CIO or IT Director – or the head of Accounts Payable – only finds out that procurement want to introduce this new system at the last minute, they're more likely to feel negative about it,' says Kleiner. It's a bit like stakeholders not involving us in Procurement until the latter stages of contracts – it doesn't make us feel well-inclined towards being helpful. So, we should apply the same principle here.

2. Be very clear about costs and timescales. 'We believe we're very honest – there are no nasty surprises, but we've seen examples where firms have been surprised by additional fees, or by the time and money needed to actually get a customised, final product delivered. Be explicit – for instance, ask directly for committed go-live dates or whether there will be supplier fees.'

3. Get beyond the formal ITT or RFP – which should itself be manageable. 'We see tender documents with over 1,000 questions for us to answer!' Often (and not surprisingly) these contain repeated questions, some irrelevant. And this can indicate a tick-box mentality generally. 'Most importantly, meet the suppliers' teams, try the platform – get behind and beyond the tick-box paper-based exercise.'

However, one final note of warning. Testing and stakeholder involvement is great, says Kleiner, but 'ultimately someone has to make a decision!' There does come a point where the elapsed time for the selection process must start cutting into the business case benefits. If it is taking you a year or more to decide… that probably means the process is simply too complex and too long.

***

But it wasn't just the new kids on the block who were coming up with exciting and innovative ideas for procurement technology. InfoNet actually morphed into other SAP Ariba products over the years, but this article identified the trend for really smart supply chain risk management software – a trend that has continued over recent years.

SAP Infonet – Genuine Innovation in Supplier Risk and Information Management

Everybody knows SAP. The granddaddy of the ERP and procurement software world. Designed for manufacturing businesses initially. Solid, inflexible, a bit slow, resource intensive in implementation terms? That is perhaps the image.

But even before the recent acquisition of Ariba, which made everybody look again at the SAP strategy, the company was changing. I read with interest my US colleague, Jason Busch, some months ago when he highlighted that SAP was innovating with surprising pace, imagination and success in the procurement space. Jason was very impressed in particular with a new SAP product, InfoNet, and I've been wanting to take a look at it ever since then.

I finally had a demo a couple of weeks ago, and one of the SAP people on the demo told me that he only recently joined the InfoNet team, and that part of his reason for doing so was reading the Jason Busch review of version 1.0 on Spend Matters US! But this is now version 2.0, and is much faster, running as it does on the new-ish SAP HANA platform, and with improved user interface. I didn't look at 1.0 so I can't verify that – but the UI certainly seemed clear and easy to use.

So, what is InfoNet? Basically, it is a supplier information, risk and performance management platform that helps you manage your supply base, measure and track performance of suppliers, and provides risk-related information and alerts about your key suppliers.

It has two particularly innovative aspects. The first is the way it allows the user to visualise multi-tier supply chains, looking not only at first-tier suppliers, but also then enabling a drill-down to sub-tiers to obtain information or alerts at the different levels. Tier 1 suppliers have to give permission for their data to be used, and they may choose to anonymise some subcontractors, but InfoNet then picks up information about their suppliers and includes that in the view available to the user.

The second innovation is in terms of where the information about suppliers comes from – there are three sources. The first is the user's own organisation. There are six standard key performance indicators (KPIs), three delivery-related and three quality-. The user maintains that KPI information about as many suppliers as they wish.

The second source is largely risk-related and comes from SAP itself. SAP is picking up news alerts about suppliers, often from source rather than waiting for things to hit the national press and provides alerts back to the user on key identified suppliers – first- or sub-tier. Alerts may relate to natural events / disasters, site disruptions, patent issues etc.

It's the third source that makes InfoNet very interesting, innovative and perhaps even unique, at the moment anyway. InfoNet also picks up data from prime contractors (tier one suppliers) and other organisations in their network who are also users of any given supplier.

That means you can compare how a supplier performs in terms of KPIs for you, versus their wider (aggregated and anonymised) network performance. That even has a forward-looking element, where InfoNet will predict, for instance, a decline in supplier performance if the system sees that supplier failing more widely.

InfoNet therefore enables the user to both look at supplier performance and manage risk better, not just at first tier but through the supply chain. It enables you to look at your entire supply chain and chart relationships – for example, where a key supplier at first tier may also be a critical second-tier supplier to other of your primes.

So, this does appear to be a genuinely innovative product, and even as a non-technophile I found it quite exciting – not something I often say about software demos! The way it is using many participants in the supply chain to gather and analyse huge amounts of information ('big data' in action) in a networked and collaborative manner may well indicate a promising future direction for procurement and supply chain technology more generally as well.

***

Back to a more general point, and Professor Richard Lamming, one of the academic gurus of my lifetime in the supply chain field.

The Supply Chain Black Box – Fantasy or Future?

Sometime ago, Professor Richard Lamming, one of the most eminent and influential procurement and supply chain academics of our time, first wrote about a somewhat provoking idea of his. In the future, he said, most of the work carried out by procurement functions would be carried out by computers. Lamming talked about 'a black box, a man and a dog'.

The black box would carry out all the routine procurement work – establishing internal requirements and specifications from internal stakeholders, talking to suppliers' black boxes to agree pricing, delivery schedules, managing the purchase-to-pay process, and so on. The man (or woman – let's not be sexist) would be there to turn on the black box every morning. And the dog was there to attack the man if he tried to turn off the black box when he shouldn't!

Now Lamming also explained that there would be a role for globetrotting dealmakers who would identify new sources of supply and manage key relationships. But the vast majority of work would be automated, and supply chain relationships would be largely black box to black box.

It's almost 10 years since I heard the professor first explaining his theories. But it's interesting to see that he is again talking about it in the context of the future of the CPO.

But is it all fantasy? Or is his vision coming to pass now? Well, to some extent. We could argue that the leading supplier and supply chain networks – Ariba, Hubwoo, Oracle, GXS, Basware – are not a million miles away from the black box vision. Certainly, the scope of activities that we can undertake in collaboration with our supply chain, without a lot of human interaction, is far greater than most of us imagined 10 years ago.

And we can perhaps see now how the next generation of artificial intelligence products will be able to take matters one step further and act appropriately on data. For instance, it might take spend analytics, payments and similar information, and work out logically what actions need to be taken, without human intervention.

The 'black box' might consider spend data by category and contact internal budget holders automatically (copy to the CFO's box) to notify of non-compliance to a corporate agreement. Or contact suppliers' black boxes to offer early payment discounts when the firm's free cash hits a certain level. That all seems quite achievable in the not too distant future.

And yet… there is a counterargument. Probably the fastest-growing firm in the supplier information management field over the last five years has been Achilles. And their unique selling proposition? Offices in 23 countries, real people who can check up on suppliers almost anywhere in the world, people who can go and physically audit factories, speak to senior staff, check on customer references. They firmly believe that a real presence on the ground is essential to obtain and verify essential information about your supply base.

I've also recently seen a practical demonstration of what is needed to facilitate a major change in P2P process. OB10, e-invoicing leaders and solution providers, were on-boarding suppliers on behalf of a huge client, that is moving its supply base onto e-invoicing.

Whilst much of the sign-up could be automated, there was still a team of effective, enthusiastic, multilingual people in the OB10 office calling suppliers, handling any issues, and generally making it happen. Now maybe that is just because the black boxes aren't as yet quite clever enough to do all of that themselves. Is it just a question of timing? And of course, even when the leading companies have their own black box, it won't be much good until most of their supply chain also has one.

I remember when the Mars Confectionery purchasing department got our first fax machine. It sat unloved in a corner for the first 12 months because we were early adopters – none of our suppliers had one!

So, is the human input simply hanging on in there, until the computers get really clever? Or will there always be a role for humans with the ability to assess complex, fluid situations and make subtle judgments? Will people always want to deal with other people?

These issues will go a long way to determining the shape and role of procurement in the future. They will also, at least in part, determine which suppliers to the procurement world are likely to succeed over the next 20 years. Should technology providers focus on making a smarter and smarter black box – or work on the assumption that there will always be human interfaces, and make the (wo)man / machine team the engine for improved performance?

***

Now, a favourite topic of mine, at the interface of leading-edge tech and leading-edge maths – but also of real practical value to procurement and organisations. A lengthy article but this is a fascinating subject.

Market Informed Sourcing – a New Paradigm for Procurement?

If you've been reading Spend Matters for a while, you'll know that the topic of 'optimisation', or advanced sourcing (or insert your favourite terminology here) has come up regularly. That's not purely because we feature the world's leading solution providers in this area amongst our sponsors, true though that is. It's more that we firmly believe that:

a. The latest technology opens up some very interesting and valuable opportunities to procurement professionals and their organisations.
b. Those opportunities are not in general well understood or used yet by the profession.

In our new White Paper on the topic, I suggest that the opportunities opened up by the latest technology actually change how procurement needs to look at one of our most fundamental processes and methodologies – that of Category Management.

I'm not suggesting that *'category management is dead'* although we did consider that as a headline-grabbing title! But I believe that for many categories, we need a fundamentally different approach, which the platforms available now will enable, and which will deliver significantly better value than current approaches.

One of the reasons that uptake of this technology has been slower than it should is confusion about the terminology. 'Optimisation' sounds a bit mathematical and obtuse. And every provider has a different term, which leads to confusion in practitioners' eyes. So, from now on, we're going to be calling this process and family of technology solutions *'market-informed sourcing'* – or *MIS* for short.

That seems the most appropriate description. Category Management has always had the benefit of a simple, fairly snappy title that everybody (consultants, practitioners etc.) uses and understands. We think that having the same commonality for this process will help drive adoption and use.

Let's look at why category management processes might not always give us the best outcomes. Imagine you're the category manager for facilities management for a large, multi-site organisation. Then in a rather larger leap of imagination, let's pretend that the Oracle (not the software firm, but the Greek source of all knowledge) is based in Hounslow. For a small fee, you can go and ask it any procurement question you like. I suspect you would go to the Oracle and say something like this:

'Hello, Oracle. Here are, in broad terms, our requirements for facilities management. Here's the list of our facilities, their size, and the type of services we need for each. These are essential services, here are the nice-to-haves. Here are our minimum service levels and we might pay a little more if someone can beat those significantly.

We have a few preferences about the sort of suppliers we want to work with as well, but we don't really mind how many suppliers we have, or whether we follow a total facilities management route or buy each service separately. Please, Oracle, tell me the best solution to my needs in terms of which suppliers should carry out which services to give me the best overall value.'

The Oracle would put down its kebab and pint of lager, and reply:

'Right, mate. There's a great, small security firm in Scotland who will do your work there, but for the rest of Europe, you should use this lot, except in France where a 'total facilities management' (TFM) deal with this firm is the best option. Catering should be split between these three firms, one of whom can also do cleaning in Southern Europe. Agreeing 3-year contracts gives you the best deal, and I reckon locking into fixed prices beats inflation linking, even though you'll pay a bit more in year one. And if you want the higher service levels it'll cost you another 8.7% – but that doesn't change the selection of suppliers much. You can decide if that's worth it.'

Thanks, Oracle.

Without the Hounslow Oracle, we tend to think about how best to structure our approach to the market through the category strategy and planning process. We think about how many suppliers we want, the structure of the supply (in this case TFM, or individual facilities services), the length of contract, the commercial mechanisms. We then dictate that to the market.

But even in the absence of an Oracle, why don't *we ask the market how it would like to meet our needs*? After all, it *must* be true that suppliers know better than us what is most economic for them and how they could best structure their supply for economic benefit. So why don't we do that?

We don't because, historically, we couldn't cope with the responses we would get from the market. Imagine going to the market for that FM contract in the way we described it to the Oracle, and getting back all sorts of options from hundreds of suppliers – how could we possibly compare them and reach a decision that optimised value for us, and was demonstrably fair and transparent to the market and colleagues?

We had to narrow down our requirement to something pretty defined, because that was the only way we could run a manageable and fair procurement process – we had to ask the suppliers to bid against a fairly narrow requirement so we could evaluate which of them should win the business.

So, driven largely by that need, what we then do is go through a process that in the White Paper I liken to a funnel. We start with our internal requirements, and our views of the markets and the suppliers within it. We narrow down our requirement until we have a nice package that we can take to market. We put a lot of work into this stage – trying to work out what is the best way of approaching the market. How many suppliers, what supply profile, the precise specification etc.

And really, when you think about it, we are trying to second-guess the market. We're trying to best determine how to structure the supply that we need – when we're never going to be as well placed as the market itself to do this. So that is the fundamental weakness of category management in most cases.

Market-informed sourcing provides an alternative. We ask the market to inform us of the best sourcing options, based on their knowledge of the true economics of the situation.

So, we ask the suppliers within that market how they would like to meet our needs. And it is clear that the market MUST understand this better than we do. And now, for the first time, the technology is powerful and clever enough to allow us to evaluate responses that are complex, disaggregated, with potentially huge numbers of fields in the responses, and offer different options and approaches.

We can explore the options, look at the lowest cost option (or build in other evaluation factors), then look at what introducing various constraints does to the price.

We could look on this as an extension of the principles of output- or outcome-based specifications – but this takes it much, much further. It enables us to hear what suppliers have always said to themselves – 'if only they could have taken our standard specification'… or 'if only they hadn't insisted on equal volumes each month'… or 'if only they hadn't wanted more volume in the US than we can currently handle …'

It enables us to explore (just as examples):

- The right number of suppliers to meet a particular need
- Regionality (e.g. a supplier who is great in Italy but does not supply to Holland)
- Seasonality of supply
- Major volume sensitivities for suppliers (e.g. big discounts if you commit to a certain purchase level, or capacity constraints)
- Flexibility around specification that is worth exploring in terms of effect on price
- Bundling and conditionality ('if you take these two products, we'll offer you an extra discount')

So, we believe that category management needs to change fundamentally – at least in the spend categories where this is particularly relevant – in order to reflect the new possibilities. The category manager needs to go to the market with an open specification and requirement – not a closed-down, precise description. This all requires a real change of mindset from professionals.

There is already evidence that even organisations that had strong and successful category management in place already are seeing significant value improvements from MIS.

So, a significant development for procurement professionals, and the organisations that can benefit from it, and we believe that practitioners, consultants, academics and everyone in the procurement ecosystem needs to be aware of the potential here.

***

But how do our suppliers feel about all this amazing new technology – not just MIS but other innovations, too? We don't tend to think too much about their feelings…

Procurement Initiatives – How Do the Suppliers Feel?

For a very long time, buyers and suppliers dealt with each other in pretty much the same way, year in, year out. The buyer sent the supplier physical tender documents, or the two parties negotiated together during face-to-face or perhaps telephone meetings. The ongoing interaction was occasional and again face-to-face or telephone-based.

We'll skim over the invention of the fax machine – although I do actually remember the excitement of realising we could send our packaging suppliers new designs instantly when faxes became ubiquitous amongst UK firms in the early 80s! But perhaps this was indicative of what was to come; I also remember telling some suppliers that they *must* get a fax if they wanted to do business with us. So that was perhaps the first time that the buyer started *dictating* a technology solution or investment to the supplier.

Through the 1980s, the rapid growth of affordable, localised computing started to change the way buyers and sellers worked together. EDI came along, and now buyers were asking – or more likely, requiring – suppliers to embrace new processes, ideas and technology. Now, of course, there are numerous examples of such processes, and buyers may require suppliers to work with them in a number of processes or activities that rely on technology, including:

- participating in sourcing events, such as e-RFx, or auctions;
- using onboarding platforms and maintaining supplier information for the buyer's use;

- accepting electronic orders, contributing to or maintaining electronic catalogues;
- participating in e-invoicing initiatives;
- signing up to supplier / buyer networks (or in some cases, more specialised 'son of EDI' approaches); and
- working with the buyer via other collaborative platforms that support closer working, better and more rapid information flow.

Many buyers, in my experience, take it for granted that their suppliers will happily sign up to these and other initiatives. The supplier can say no, but not many choose to do so. However, as we move into a world where some key commodities, raw materials or components may be in short supply, it is worth remembering that suppliers do have a choice. It is likely that becoming a 'customer of choice' will be an important objective for many organisations and procurement functions.

So, what should buyers be considering in order to sell the benefits of embracing process or technology change to their supply base? (And these are, of course, also valid points that technology *providers* should remember, even if they're primarily making their sale to the buyers, not the suppliers.) What do suppliers look for and think about when the buyer introduces a new requirement, and what benefits might they perceive?

Clearly, the supplier will be positive if they see this as a real opportunity to *increase their business with the buyer*. Often the buyer positions it more as an avoided negative – 'if you don't agree to use our e-sourcing platform, you won't be able to bid for our work'. But turning that around into a positive is a more motivating way perhaps of presenting this. 'Using our e-sourcing system will give you access to bid for our work.'

A slight variation of this is the opportunity to *win more business with the wider customer organisation* – maybe beyond the current individual buyer / unit / cost centre. So systemising supplier information, for example, may lead to the whole buying organisation being aware of a good supplier that is currently only serving one part of the organisation. That can be a major positive for the supplier.

On other occasions, it may be that the technology gives the supplier *access to totally new business* with totally new buyers. The Ariba Discovery product is a good example of that – 'sign up to our platform and we'll give you access to customers you've never even heard of' is essentially the pitch there.

In a somewhat different manner, pre-qualification platforms like Achilles can provide suppliers access to buyers in a particular industry that they may not currently count as customers. So, a single customer can present that as an opportunity to the supplier, even if the realisation of that opportunity is going to come from other buyers.

A further benefit for the supplier can arise from their own *efficiency savings*. An effective supplier network, allied with e-invoicing processes, can, for instance, reduce the cost to the supplier of the whole end-to-end transactional purchase-to-pay process, from receiving purchase orders, getting them to the right person, invoicing, chasing payment, funding the late payment… and so on.

The subject of supplier payment for network activities is a contentious one; but whether and how the supplier pays, selling the benefits to the supply side is a sensible move for buyers to take. Both in terms of relationships and minimising any future price increases (as suppliers look to compensate for their higher costs), it is much better for the buyer to present the positives to the supplier rather than simply issuing an ultimatum – 'join the network or else!'

A benefit to suppliers can also arise through the opportunity to *develop a relationship or an improved relationship* with the buyer. This factor is being emphasised by both network providers and, increasingly, through more niche technology products. Suppliers (and buyers) may perceive a value to that, through less friction in the working relationship and perhaps the chance of building further business volume and value.

Those are the main factors to consider, but our general point is that, ultimately, the supplier will make their own assessment of the benefit – or otherwise – they gain from their involvement in the new technology or process. If the buyer is powerful and the supplier needs to preserve the business, they may continue to participate even if they don't see the change as a positive step forward. If the result of process changes or new technology is simply an additional cost being loaded onto the supplier, they will in most cases find a way of recovering margin elsewhere.

So clearly, if the buyer can demonstrate that the supplier will actually *gain* from their involvement, there is more chance of a co-operative approach, better value from the supplier, a harmonious relationship, and a happy supply base.

***

But what are the tech providers really trying to do – make our lives easier or give us more and more complex but clever products?

Simplification Versus Functionality – the Battle for Sourcing Solution Primacy

When we look at developments in sourcing software, there are two strong trends that at first sight appear to be moving the market in opposite directions. As we'll see, that is not strictly true, but these developments reflect quite different drivers in the marketplace, to which providers are responding in their own ways.

I should stress at this stage that this isn't going to be a highly technical discussion – my interest lies in what the software direction suggests about the role of the procurement function and the implications for senior procurement leaders, rather than the detail of technology strategies.

The first trend is for ever-increasing ease of use for software – not necessarily simplification from the point of view of functionality, but presenting an easier, simpler interface to the user. This responds to the digital natives coming into the workforce, who don't expect to read a manual, let alone go on a training course before they use any software. Logon, then find the app or website and 'start doing stuff', is their expectation.

Yet, at the same time, the other meta-trend in sourcing is the growth of firms such as CombineNet – acquired recently by SciQuest – and Trade Extensions. They are thriving with significant growth in demand for their solutions, which support the most complex sourcing exercises and challenges. There is a growing appetite amongst (in the main) larger organisations for the capabilities to address the most difficult procurement tasks, with many variables and huge amounts of data to analyse, in a manner that can deliver considerable value.

Now those software firms have put effort into making their platforms easier to use, but no one is likely to suggest that using such products is anything like as simple as the products from firms who major on that aspect. So, is this a paradox?

The market, we might argue, does not like paradox. The answer must be no – it is merely an example of different market drivers, and needs, moving in different directions, with different firms fulfilling these needs. What we are seeing is two different trends, that are not in reality pulling in opposite directions – it's more a case of looking at a picture from two different angles. And that picture shows a differentiation, even within one organisation, between sourcing tasks of different types and natures.

But all these developments have one common driver – increases in technology capacity and capability. User-friendliness actually needs significant processing power to support design features that contribute to ease of use (such as user prompts, drop-down menus, applications that learn from previous user experience). And the computing power needed to run complex optimisation algorithms is very obvious.

So, one trend is making technology easier principally to benefit the casual user, who needs to 'do some buying' from time to time. The other trend is using greater power to provide services that previously weren't possible at all – we have also written previously about how optimisation / market-informed sourcing offers an alternative to traditional category management that just wasn't feasible until processing got cheaper.

Those services based on complexity tend to be first taken up by experts until the general user both catches on and the cost comes down to a mass market level. For example, the first systems for searching for flights were purely the preserve of travel agents and airlines – then eventually became the websites we all use without thinking. And the same is likely to happen with complex sourcing – it will eventually spread both across organisations, and deeper within those that have already adopted it.

Implications for the procurement function
So firstly, what are the implications for the procurement function in terms of their relationship with internal stakeholders? Let's take the user-friendly aspect first. Is it positive for procurement functions

if budget holders can run and understand tendering processes themselves?

It's not clear yet what appetite users will have for running their own processes. Just because it can be done doesn't mean it will be, and much may depend on the current service that they receive from procurement. We can imagine users may be delighted to simply get on with things themselves in organisations where procurement is not very responsive.

It also depends on how far procurement activity covers 'tail spend' – lower value requirements. So, in many cases, we may see use of these platforms replacing paper- or email-driven, amateur procurement processes. In such cases, we would expect users to welcome some assistance and the organisation should see the development as positive.

But the risk for procurement is that users may get the appetite for running sourcing processes. Some of the mystique of competitive bidding processes, setting evaluation factors, scoring bids and so on, may fade if the technology helps and educates users to understand the processes.

It's also possible that users (and indeed procurement users) may quickly see the benefit of effective sourcing and systems to support it, but see limitations in the easy to use products. One market leading provider of sourcing solutions told me recently: 'Once the entry-level customers try a basic product and get used to the principle of e-sourcing, they will quickly want to upgrade to something like our product when they start to appreciate what the additional functionality can bring.'

That feels to me more like an argument that will apply to procurement users rather than budget holders, who are more likely to be satisfied with something that delivers 80% of the capability quickly and easily.

Implications for the market (suppliers)

Is it possible that the same provider could supply the full range of sourcing platforms? A simple to use product with the core functionality that a non-expert and probably non-procurement professional user might use for lower value, non-critical sourcing exercises, perhaps a mid-range product for much conventional, procurement-led tenders, and an optimisation-type top-end platform for those really complex spend areas?

Well, it's not impossible, but I suspect it is harder than it looks and whether a single firm can have such different sourcing DNAs all working within their corporate bodies, I'm not sure. *(Late news – Coupa, whose initial pitch was all about simplicity, bought Trade Extensions with their top of the range sourcing capability in 2017, so I think I was wrong here – the answer was, 'Yes, we will see the same firm offering a range of options!')*

Implications for consultants

One other group of people needs to be aware of these trends, too. It was interesting to note that A.T. Kearney in the book written by four of their consultants featured optimisation as one of the key techniques. Perhaps they have seen that the mystique of running what are now standard category management and sourcing processes has gone, so they have to stay ahead of the curve. And as software gets both more powerful and easier to use, they will have to keep that jump ahead of clients to show they can add value in what they bring to the party.

***

There is an irony in our next piece, in that it followed criticism from a reader that I was writing too much about 'small' solution providers.

Such as… Coupa. That firm's growth since this was written explains well why Spend Matters covered and still covers solution providers both large and small. By the way, I was right about Ben Howard, half right about Django Django, and wrong about Natalie Duncan!

Why Write About 'Small' Procurement Solutions Providers?

We got a very interesting comment at the weekend that I wanted to answer directly. Daniele Brione has a bit of a go at us for covering smaller firms (Proactis, Wax, Coupa) – with the suggestion that they are businesses whose market cap / size / results 'don't suggest that Ariba or SAP should hold out too much concern'. Brione went on to say, 'My only question is why these firms are given so much credit in these pages given the numerical realities?'

That's a really good question, actually. So here we go with honest answers!

1. Biggest reason – it would be really, really boring if we only wrote about the big firms all the time. Boring to write about, boring to read. That's why the music magazines don't just feature Lady Gaga or Rihanna every week. Or the car mags the Ford Focus. I like writing about stuff that I find interesting, new, exciting. Sometimes that is SAP – as per the InfoNet review the other day, a product I think is really innovative – sometimes it is some much smaller firm. That's an open invitation, by the way – if you have an exciting, innovative product / solution / idea, let us know!

2. Linked to that, anyone who writes about a particular interest area tends to get excited about the new stuff – using the music analogy again, trying to spot the next Lady Gaga (Ben Howard is on the road

to greatness; look out for Natalie Duncan perhaps and Django Django will be huge...) is more fun for reader and writer than just more of the same. Coupa are growing like mad and we do think they're probably a mega-player of the future (unless they get bought first).

3. You can't just take market capitalisation as an indicator of interest. You can have a small market cap but actually quite a large installed base of interested customers – I'd put Proactis into that category, for instance. And while SAP have a huge market cap, of course procurement is only one relatively small element of their total portfolio. Sure, they are big in procurement, but they're not the only game in town. So, we're simply trying to cover the bases for all our readers.

4. However, I'd point out that we (Spend Matters US and our new PRO site) have probably written around 20,000 words on the SAP / Ariba deal, its consequences, the products, the strategy etc. We're not exactly underplaying the 'big boys'!

5. Finally, while we do write genuinely very independently, of course we think we're going to get more chance of sponsorship and revenue if we cover a wide field of providers. It's not the main reason – that is the 'boredom factor' above. But yes, we think it's commercially sensible to range widely across providers. Having said that, the three smaller firms mentioned have not paid Spend Matters UK/Europe a penny to date!

Thanks for the question anyway – and if there are other people you think we should be covering, do let us know.

***

Not all the software firms we wrote about thrived, of course. The story of the IBM acquisition of Emptoris is a sad one. IBM was not able to make a success of it, and the Emptoris name and product are now defunct. But it all looked so promising at first. And when I said, 'It's easy to see how a more "local" competitor to Xcitec might develop some positioning to go after Xcitec clients,' riskmethods didn't even exist! But even before the final demise of Emptoris, riskmethods and others were eating into their business.

Further Thoughts on IBM / Emptoris

It was interesting to see that the contract Emptoris won with the UK Government – for their sourcing tool – was given such prominence in the IBM acquisition announcement. It is important, without a doubt, but it will be interesting to see how the team at the Government Procurement Service perceive this move. IBM has had some recent poor publicity in terms of public procurement, and the mood in Cabinet Office is very much in favour of small, agile, open source-type IT strategies and suppliers, which suggests IBM would not necessarily be flavour of the month.

In addition, it was John Collington (now Government CPO), when he was at the Home Office, who was the first big supporter of Emptoris in government circles. I believe that was based on his experience working with them when he was at Accenture – with whom Emptoris has always had a close relationship.

How will Collington feel about Accenture's number 1 competitor now owning Emptoris? Cleary, this isn't going to jeopardise the recent deal or anything, but as the precise scope and therefore potential revenue from this contract are still up for grabs, perceptions might matter. If they are smart, IBM will make sure they retain the key Emptoris people who have built those government relationships.

Secondly, the Xcitec (risk management) acquisition a few months ago brought strong capability (and some good people) into the Emptoris fold. But Xcitec strike me as a quite Germany-centric firm. Their client base was (and still is, I believe) heavily centred around large German corporates. Now those clients have already seen the move to Emptoris – but now seeing Xcitec swallowed up by arguably the most American of all tech firms – how will they respond? It's easy to see how a more 'local' competitor to Xcitec might develop some positioning to go after Xcitec clients.

Xcitec was also allowing Emptoris to develop an interesting positioning around 'supplier life-cycle management'. But this was based strongly on a holistic view of their capability. Now, if that positioning gets changed with additional IBM products brought into the mix, the logic may get less clear.

We should stress that there are of course many potential positives with the deal. IBM has a great opportunity to show in Europe that they really are experts in procurement – in consulting, in software and in outsourced service provision. I've been a huge admirer for many years of how they run their own procurement, but they have not in my view ever quite exploited that as well as they might in third-party sales terms.

Emptoris gives the firm a great opportunity to build its leadership positioning in these markets – but there are risks ahead as well, including those we've described.

***

Chapter 3

CURRENT AFFAIRS

I have always enjoyed commenting on what was going on in the wider world, often including those events that didn't immediately seem to have a connection with procurement and supply chain management.

In fact, if I would claim to have any unique skill, it is in seeing a procurement 'angle' in the most unlikely of places, such as the selection of the shortlist for the BBC Sports Personality of the Year! Or indeed, a tragic shooting in Washington, DC.

So, in this section, you will find a really very wide range of topics, including the two above, as well as fish, the Crystal Methodist, Olympic hotel prices and the meaning of Dubai. And if you start looking, you can find a procurement angle in almost everything you see. Just try it!

The Crystal Methodist

What can we say about the Crystal Methodist, the Rev. Flowers? Is there a procurement angle that gives me the excuse to write about a story that if you read it as a novel, you would classify as 'magical realism' rather than anything likely to happen in real life?

But here we have a senior councillor, school governor and ultimately a director and Chairman of the Co-operative Bank who turned out to have a predilection for hard drugs, porn, and ketamine-fuelled rent boy orgies. And he looks like such a nice man, too. So, let's try and draw a few vaguely procurement-related thoughts from this.

1. Don't trust appearances. Many people go into public life because they want to contribute to the greater good and make a difference.

A few do it in order to do bad things (corruption). And a very few may do it to camouflage their failings. Who would suspect a Minister, and Councillor, of having a dissolute and wild personality? So, whether it is in suppliers, colleagues or friends, look beyond the smart and conforming appearance to the person beneath …

2. On a related note, there is a great deal of faith being placed by politicians (of both parties) in institutions such as charities, mutuals, not-for-profits, or community interest companies. There is an assumption – when we see them talking about doing good works – that they must be 'good things'. Procurement is getting caught up in this, too, encouraged to give more business to this sort of organisation. But again, appearances can be deceptive. The Chairman of the Co-operative Bank, for goodness' sake. It's like hearing that Father Christmas is getting too friendly with Rudolph! Let's be positively cautious about these organisations: don't assume they're all full of good people all doing good things.

3. Politics and business are almost always a toxic mix when they get too close. The Co-op Bank has lent millions of pounds to the Labour Party, and the appointment of Flowers as Chair seems to have been driven by his political connections more than his banking credibility. Credit to the Tories for avoiding any business-related scandals in this administration – the Grant Shapps affair never quite achieved take-off in the public eyes.

4. And that need for separation between politics and business is another reason we have to be diligent in public procurement – and yes, occasionally put up with a bit of EU regulatory nonsense – in order to make sure public procurement never becomes just a branch of politics, privilege and patronage (as it still is in too many

countries, unfortunately).

Finally, as a procurement person, it is also good to get a bit of market intelligence on a tricky spend category. So, thanks to The Reverend, I now have a much better idea of what it will cost me for my next drug-fuelled night with rent boys in Leeds. (Only joking, of course…)

***

On a much more serious note, the growth of corporate social responsibility over recent years has been a major issue for procurement as we try to get more involved in what our suppliers and supply chains are doing. The Rana Plaza disaster was to some extent a wake-up call for buyers of cheap clothing, although a few years on, I'm not sure that much has really changed.

Rana Plaza Disaster – How Should Buyers Respond?

Despite the amazing story of the young woman rescued from the rubble after 17 days, the shocking death toll from the Rana Plaza Bangladesh factory collapse is now up to around 1050. To put that in perspective, that is more than died in the South Tower of the World Trade Center on September 11th, 2001.

Some of the Western firms who have subcontractors operating in Bangladesh are beginning to announce longer-term responses to the tragedy. Disney, for instance, have announced they will stop production of branded merchandise in the country, although that seems to have been decided just before this latest disaster, and they are also pulling out of Ecuador, Venezuela, Belarus and Pakistan by April 2014.

According to CNN, 'The company said its decision was based

on a report from the World Bank that assesses how countries are governed, using metrics like accountability, corruption and violence, among others. The five countries from which Disney pulled production had the lowest scores on those measures.'

It is likely that other firms may make similar decisions, based on reputational risk, but there is another side to that argument. The Bangladeshi Nobel Peace Prize winner, Muhammad Yunus, who developed the concepts of microfinance and microcredit, wrote in an article published by newspapers in the country last week that the disaster was 'a symbol of our failure as a nation'.

> The crack in Rana Plaza that caused the collapse of the building has only shown us that if we don't face up to the cracks in our state systems, we as a nation will get lost in the debris of the collapse,' he added. But he urged buyers not to abandon the country. Rather, he wants firms from more developed countries to treat workers in their subcontractor firms as 'de facto employees.

Now maybe that is too much to expect – I don't see Western firms extending pension provision, paid sick leave and so on to staff in those supplier firms. But in terms of basic protection around issues such as health and safety, working hours and conditions, then yes, that may increasingly be the way firms need to look at it.

But as we've said before, this needs a change of attitude in a number of ways. It needs firms to move away – even if it is only slightly – from the unrelenting focus on driving down costs we've seen over recent years. The whole drive to sell T-shirts for 99p or a couple of dollars would need to change (which of course raises issues quite fundamental to the whole nature of capitalism, we might argue).

Indeed, a UK trade union claimed this week that if the retailers were prepared to pay just 2p more – 3 cents or so – per garment, then that would allow the wages of the Bangladeshi employees in the relevant factories to double. Assuming that is an accurate analysis, it is certainly something for Western buyers to consider.

Addressing these issues also needs buyers to have a better understanding of their supply chains and suppliers than many have today. The first step towards doing anything positive for the workers in these firms is for the customers to actually know and understand who is doing what for them in their supply chains. Without that knowledge, nothing can be achieved.

But often, the web of contractors, subcontractors and sub-subcontractors is complex and opaque. It's no wonder many buyers give up and just hope for the best in terms of their supply chain risk strategies. That suggests that there is more potential also for solution providers who can help firms understand better these complex supply chains and networks.

We suspect this requirement will continue and grow, with more call for proactive supplier assessments and certifications, rather than simply collecting supplier-provided data. We also expect solutions which rely on collecting supplier information from a number of sources, including from other customers, as well as via local news items and market intelligence, to increase their penetration in the market as buyers become more concerned and demanding in terms of real-time, accurate and meaningful information.

As Muhammad Yunus explained, there are real dangers to Bangladesh if buyers do simply pull out of the country altogether. That would probably weaken the Bangladesh economy further, pushing business there into taking even more shortcuts to reduce costs. Fewer blue-chip customers might also take away some of the positive pressure to improve their own practices that those firms can bring to bear.

So greater engagement by Western buyers, to help the country and the suppliers within it to improve standards for workers, is the better outcome that we might hope for. That could at least bring some positive results from this tragedy.

***

If that story wasn't depressing enough, let's have a bit of US-style mass shooting; but with a quite surprising 'supply chain' background.

Aaron Alexis – a Tragic Side to Corporate Virtualisation

Thirty years ago, we would suspect that all or the vast majority of the IT staff working on a sensitive military site in the US or the UK would have been employed directly by the military authorities. Following the first major wave of IT outsourcing in the late-1980s and early 90s, the chances are that many would have been working for a large outsourced service provider – an IBM, HP (EDS), CSC, or Accenture maybe.

This week, we heard and saw much too much about an IT worker, Aaron Alexis, who was an independent contractor, working for what appears to be a respected and major IT services firm in the US called The Experts, who were working under contract to Hewlett-Packard, who were themselves under contract to the US Navy.

'Aaron Alexis was an employee of a company called 'The Experts,' a subcontractor to an HP Enterprise Services contract to refresh equipment used on the navy marine corps intranet (NMCI) network. HP is cooperating fully with law enforcement as requested.'

Alexis, for reasons we don't yet understand, on Monday shot 12 people dead at the Navy Yard in Washington, DC, in the USA.

What a tragic demonstration of the trend identified in the Proxima report that we've featured recently. 'Corporate Virtualization –

A global study of cost externalization and its implications on profitability' shows that the average organisation spends 69.6% of its revenues with suppliers now, compared to just 12.5% on staff costs.

Of course, much of this external spend is, in reality, people. People doing IT work; cleaning or catering tasks; project managers or consultants; external lawyers, window cleaners or security guards. And many of these will at some stage be working on the client's premises.

'What was once a payslip is now a supplier invoice,' as the report puts it. And this tragic example highlights that not only are firms now buying services they might once have carried out in-house, but the firms to whom they give the contracts (the prime contractors) are also often subcontracting themselves, creating longer and more complex supply chains and networks.

Now, of course, that does not in itself increase the possibility of tragedies such as this. There have always been examples of angry, evil or disturbed employees committing terrible crimes. But this move to the 'virtualised organisation' brings some new challenges for the ultimate client.

There is some suggestion in reports that Alexis may have been angry about a perceived issue over payment and money he felt his firm owed him. (Now we should stress this is just hearsay and there may be no truth in it.) However, that does highlight one issue – even if it proves to be a red herring here – how does the ultimate client know that the people who are working for them (in some sense) are motivated, positively aligned and capable, when they don't have that direct employment relationship?

Now there are other issues here around security clearance processes, the past history of the gunman, gun control of course, and so on. But this is a tragic example of a supply chain risk that we might not have even imagined once upon a time. It also emphasises again those issues around the importance of contract and supplier management that we frequently feature, and the need to consider suppliers and their staff (in some ways at least) as you would your own staff.

Finally, and most importantly, our sincere condolences to everyone who has been affected, and good wishes for recovery for those injured this week.

***

Now, a particular bugbear of mine – why do firms allow their investment bankers and corporate advisers to charge such ridiculously high fees? That's followed by thoughts on one takeover that did go through, as Kraft swallowed up the great British firm, Cadbury.

Bankers Bonuses, Purchasing Problems, and a Campaign

The big news is that the UK government has announced it will tax bankers' bonuses at 50%; a measure supported by most of the public (but unsurprisingly, not by many bankers). It looks like France may follow, but in Germany Angela Merkel says she thinks it is a 'charming idea', which we understand is German shorthand for, 'we have to show some support for our EU comrades but we will also be delighted if disaffected bankers would like to relocate to lovely, charming, dynamic, exciting Frankfurt, our own competitor to horrible, smelly, crowded, inefficient old London.'

What does this have to do with purchasing? Well, I asked some time ago (in response to a *London Evening Standard* article) whether clients of the banking and finance industry are at least partly to blame for the huge earnings in that industry, and some of the consequent problems.

The Times last week featured another piece on the topic; big investors are 'preparing an assault on the 'exorbitant' fees of advisers on both sides of company takeovers'. These fees are apparently around 3% of the value of the takeover; so that is 3% of the total shareholder value gone just like that … and of course we are often talking about billion-dollar values here. As *The Times* reports:

> One investor said: 'It is egregious. The pensions and savings of our customers are being used to pay ludicrous investment banking fees, which are leading to supernormal profits at the banks and then leaving the door as excessive bonuses.'

As a purchasing person, the obvious question is: why do the buying organisations allow this to happen? Firms don't allow suppliers of any other service to rip them off so obviously. Our cleaning contractor – or even our strategic consulting adviser – would be greeted by hysterical laughter if they demanded 3% of the company's value in return for doing a few weeks' work.

For a start, there is no reason at all why the fees should be linked to the size of the deal – that is totally illogical. The amount of work is not related to that, so why would we accept a payment mechanism of that nature? And what about competition? Why doesn't that drive down the fees to something more economically justified?

The reason of course is that competitive processes are almost unheard of in this industry. And professional purchasing people rarely get close to the process; there is no opportunity for us to apply our processes and discipline. This is a failure of procurement – a failure of procurement governance, process, the credibility of our profession.

And once competition is neutered, as we all know, cartel-like behaviour becomes much more likely in any market. Not that I would suggest anything illegal here for a moment, but it is interesting how quickly something like this 3% fee becomes the 'norm'.

So why do CEOs and Chairmen act in this way and agree these deals? It is partly the genuine concerns around time and confidentiality: you can't hold off defending the takeover while the purchasing department runs a 3-month tendering process. But that could be addressed by putting in place prearranged agreements. It is also I'm sure the Board's genuine belief that they must have the firm or people they believe are 'the best'. If they are defending the whole future of the organisation, paying a few tens of millions to the advisers is the least of their worries and seems a 'fair' price to pay.

But their definition of 'the best' often means nothing more than they've worked with them before, or they play golf together. That leads us into what we could define uncharitably as corruption. The trips to sporting events, the opera or ballet for the older chief executives and the strip clubs at the younger end of the market, the Christmas hampers, the lucrative consulting assignment or non-executive role offered with the advising bank once the Chairman steps down ... All unethical, and quite possibly tipping over into corruption.

So, what can be done? My suggestion is that we start a Campaign for Proper Purchasing of Investment Banking Services (CPPIBS – so the acronym needs a bit of work) I am sure we could get buy-in from investors' bodies and others (maybe even Government), to implement either laws or at least strong guidelines, that would enshrine proper purchasing and governance into these decisions.

And I think we would only need three key statements to make a real difference.

1. Organisations will put in place and publish their procurement policies and processes, which will be applied to all external expenditure, including spend that falls into this 'City' or banking category.

2. Everyone in an organisation who is involved in spending money with suppliers will sign up to the Institute for Supply Management (ISM) or Chartered Institute of Procurement and Supply (CIPS) ethical code, as many buyers already do. The Code sensibly defines what is and is not acceptable around gifts, hospitality, and so on. And no, hampers are not allowed. Board hospitality will be declared in the published annual corporate accounts.

3. All expenditure over a certain level – say $100,000 – including banking and related fees, will go through some competitive process before a contract is put in place (with any exceptions to be listed in the annual report).

Is this workable? Shall we start the campaign?

***

Cadbury / Kraft Hope for Procurement Savings

I spent the first 10 years of my career in the food industry, so the recent takeover of Cadbury by Kraft was particularly interesting. Apart from a general sadness that another major British food company has gone (and there ain't many left) I was interested in a comment by the Kraft CEO now that there won't need to be big staff reductions because they will make huge savings from better procurement.

As well as my general cynicism about savings measurement and credibility, that brought to mind some of my personal experience in the food industry in the 80s (and since) around the issue of economies of scale. And that was where I formed the view that economy of scale is one of the biggest myths in the procurement world.

Now, I don't deny that in many industries and for many purchases, economies of scale do apply up to a point. Clearly, as a buyer, I want and need to have some market power which volume does bring. But too many people assume that the economy of scale curve continues indefinitely; that the more volume I buy, the better the price I will obtain. This is simply not true in all category areas.

I had direct experience of this in the food industry. I bought flour (amongst other raw materials) for a couple of years. I was a big buyer but not one of the giants in the market, the bread makers and the top biscuit manufacturers. But I knew that we got better prices than most – if not all – of the bigger users. Why?

Simply, we could move faster, be more entrepreneurial and take more risk. If you need hundreds of tons of flour a day, you can't take supply risks. You must have guaranteed supply, you need to lock it in some way ahead, and you may well be buying 50% or more of a flour mill's entire output. The mill cannot supply you on a marginal pricing basis when their whole business depends on you. As a friend pointed out to me, 'If you buy a supplier's entire output, you must be paying the average price.'

We bought tactically and aggressively. A long list of approved suppliers, and a quarterly price competition (before the days of e-auctions but the same principle). And we bought enough quantity to be interesting to suppliers, but not so much that they couldn't afford to offer us marginal volume at marginal pricing. I have heard similar stories in other markets; for instance, the group of airlines who failed to get a great deal from hotels at an airport because their combined volume was just too much.

A friend who until recently worked for one of the largest food firms in the world also confirmed that when you are the major global buyer in a raw material market, you do not necessarily get 'the best prices'. Other factors such as security of supply go to the top of the priority list.

So, Kraft / Cadbury will need to be careful. Maintaining agility in their combined supply chains will be key to generating savings, not merely relying on volume and economies of scale. Of course, we'll never know the truth, as no doubt in a couple of years' time Kraft will declare how tremendously successful the initiative has been, but without any public evidence. (A favourite topic again – the unreliably of procurement savings numbers.) But let's hope they are genuine and great procurement does turn out to mitigate the need for job cuts.

***

After some depressing and serious stuff, the next selection of short pieces brings together some of my lighter commentary on the world and its tenuous procurement connections. Let's hear it for Gareth Bale, fish provenance, condoms, and Japanese mummies. And that's a sentence you don't read very often.

Gareth Bale and Spurs' BATNA

I smiled when I heard football club Tottenham Hotspur (Spurs) claiming this week that another club was interested in buying Gareth Bale. Note to readers who aren't football fans – don't stop reading! This isn't really an article about football!

It appears that Spurs and Real Madrid are in the final stages of negotiation over Bale's transfer, with the fee likely to be around £80 million. Everyone seems pretty certain it will happen, so there was some surprise at this new interest from elsewhere. An unspecified and non-specific 'elsewhere' also …

But as procurement professionals, we can of course see exactly what Spurs are doing. They are improving the strength of their

BATNA – the best alternative to a negotiated agreement, as defined by Fisher and Ury in their seminal negotiation book, *Getting to Yes*. They are, in effect, saying to Real Madrid that they have decent alternatives, including someone else who is interested in paying stupid amounts of money for the player.

Having a good, strong BATNA plays a huge part in defining the strength of your negotiation position. Suppose it was well known that no one else was remotely interested in Bale. Suppose – an even more extreme example – that Spurs desperately needed the cash as well (absolutely not true in real life!) But in that situation, how would Spurs BATNA look? Really not very strong, and the fee being discussed would not be anywhere like £80m.

But the other interesting point is that it isn't *really* how good your BATNA is – what's critical is how good the other party *thinks* it is. So, it is interesting that we don't know who this other party ready to jump in really is. Of course, Spurs wouldn't just invent this other bid, would they? But the key thing from a negotiation point of view is that Real Madrid believes, or at least has a reasonable suspicion, that Spurs actually do have a feasible alternative – the BATNA. That keeps some negotiating power in Spurs' hands.

So, there we go – another nice example of the principles and practices of procurement coming into our lives and the national news. But let's not get into the value for money issues around paying £80m for a guy who has basically had one good season in the Premiership ...!

(Note – Bale proved to be a pretty good buy for Real, we'd argue.)

***

No Cod? OK, Pufferfish and Chips Please

Whatever next? An analysis of fish samples in US outlets showed that a third weren't actually the fish they claimed to be. Here's the SFGate website (from San Francisco):

'Genetic testing of 1,215 fish taken from 674 retail outlets, grocery stores and sushi bars throughout the United States between 2010 and 2012 found that 33 percent of the samples had been mislabelled, according to U.S. Food and Drug Administration guidelines.'

Fish labelled as snapper turned out to be rockfish, and white tuna was actually escolar, which has a well-known laxative effect. Pennsylvania was the worst State with 56% of the tested fish turning out to be something other than what was described on the label or menu.

The worry really is that once you lose trust in your suppliers and supply chains, it calls all sorts of things into question. We might laugh at the laxative example given in the fish story but not at this: serious illnesses have occurred in the past, most notably in 2007 when toxic pufferfish were mislabelled as monkfish in an attempt to circumvent US import restrictions, according to the FDA.

Or when adulterated milk powder cost children's lives in China, or (just as a theoretical example) if counterfeit components caused disaster when used in a plane, train or bus.

So, is this current scandal going to blow over and be forgotten – or is it going to lead to some fundamental changes in the way supply chains work? I wonder. But in any case, it highlights again a whole range of questions for procurement people and indeed everyone.

- How do we know what we're really eating in restaurants?
- How do we know what is going into the food we buy in shops?

- How do we know that our suppliers are providing exactly what they say they are?
- How do we know that our suppliers' suppliers are doing the same?
- How do we check and verify what we're told by our suppliers we're getting?
- How often is it really feasible to do that sort of checking, given cost and resource issues?
- What actions do we take if we find out we didn't get what we specified / ordered / bought?

And most importantly – when I order Cod and Chips, how do I know it's REALLY Cod?!

**

Durex are 'Condomed' to Procurement and Supply Chain Problems (sorry ...)

Last week a great story broke that not only features sex, but also includes elements of supply chain risk, offshoring strategies, partnership and strategic relationship management, power in the supply chain, merger and acquisition risk; it's virtually a year's worth of *Harvard Business Reviews* all in one case study!

So, SSL, makers of Durex condoms, was acquired recently by Reckitt Benckiser for $3.9 billion. A large percentage of their products are actually manufactured in India by TTK, with whom SSL have a joint venture. (I don't know the precise terms of that venture.)

But, as the *Economic Times* reports, a dispute started shortly after the takeover when TTK tried to implement a 35% price increase for condoms destined for the international market. TTK also wanted to lock Reckitt Benckiser into a 5-year supply contract.

In an interim court ruling, TTK were told to keep supplying, at the higher price, until the dispute was resolved. But they've refused to do even that, so in a filing in the Chennai High Court, Reckitt has accused TTK of contempt of court. The Court has given TTK until November 8 to explain why they haven't complied with the first order.

In the meantime, Reckitt is buying more condoms 'at high prices', according to reports from suppliers in China and Thailand. (Guys – you all happy with the quality control issues here? I'm sure they'll be fine. Absolutely fine.)

TTK is concerned that Reckitt intends to replace it as a supplier with new factories that Reckitt is building in China. So, here's a bit of free consulting for TTK – cutting off supply is not usually, in my experience, a great way of persuading customers that they should keep on relying on you as a supplier. That's really going to make Reckitt say, 'I tell you what, let's not bother with the new factory. Let's just keep buying from those nice, reliable people at TTK...'

Professor Andrew Cox must be writing a case study now – his seminal work on power in supply chains came to mind as soon as I read this. Who holds the power here? TTK in the short term, Reckitt in the longer, I suspect, assuming there are other reasonable suppliers around. We might also see this as a sign of some changing dynamics – Indian companies becoming more assertive perhaps? Cost pressures in countries like India working through to Western buyers?

And a spokesperson for the NHS Supply Chain in the UK, said, 'NHS Supply Chain is continuing to manage the situation by offering customers suitable alternative products from other suppliers on the framework agreement to ensure that there is minimum disruption to services; please note that not all products in this range have been affected.' (I didn't even know we could get condoms on the NHS.)

Anyway, there is apparently no shortage of condoms, yet, in Europe. So, you can all rest easy in your beds tonight. Or don't rest, if you see what I mean.

***

Japanese Mummies and Savings Measurement

OK, so if that heading didn't attract your interest, then there is no hope for my writing skills.

I've been writing a series of pieces on procurement savings, including how to 'capture' those savings. And that issue, of how to turn a theoretical saving into something real that contributes to profit or is genuinely reused in a productive manner, is just one of the reasons why I am very cynical about most of the savings claims made by procurement people and increasingly by organisations in their annual reports, acquisition documents, and so on. You know the sort of thing.

'Merger benefits will include $500 million from combining purchasing and greater buying power'. Or 'Procurement savings of £100m this year contributed to record profits'.

The truth is that, unless you know what methodology for measuring and capturing savings (or for predicting future savings) has been used, we can have no clue as to how accurate or even vaguely credible they might be.

It isn't long ago that Supply Management was featuring the great performance of ITV's procurement function. Now suddenly, the Director is leaving. This is no criticism of the magazine, ITV or the lady in question, and clearly I don't know the full story. But one can't help wondering whether there was a mismatch between how procurement was reporting its achievements, and how it was perceived by top management. Savings numbers – or any numbers – never tell the whole story. And that takes us into the mummified Japanese story.

We've been told for years now about the amazing longevity of the Japanese race. More centurions than any other country. Now *The Times* reports an amazing story, that this appears to have been an illusion based on appalling report keeping, non-existent social services, and greedy 'children' (themselves of pensionable age) concealing their parent's death to carry on claiming their pensions and benefits. Often the actual body was also concealed – hence the mummification! Here's a sample from *The Times*.

> The plan was simple: knock on Sogen Kato's front door, congratulate him on his longevity, offer a cash reward and inquire whether Tokyo's oldest resident would, at the age of 111, mind taking part in Japan's 'Respect the Elderly' festivities on September 20.

But after a few issues with his 81-year-old daughter, the authorities were finally led upstairs to Kato's bedroom. He was there – well, his mummified body was, bones swaddled in bandages and surrounded by newspapers from October 1978, which turned out to be the actual time he had passed away. His daughter had been claiming his pension ever since then of course.

The moral of the story is – don't take 'information' and 'facts' on trust. Ask to see the raw data. Ask where it comes from. How is it verified? Could it be distorted? Does the person communicating with you have a vested interest in the data? These are great questions to bear in mind, whether it is in dealings with suppliers, in reading the newspapers, in listening to politicians – or even when reading procurement articles.

***

I travelled to Dubai around 10 times from 2012 to 2017 to run workshops with software firm Tejari. They were fascinating (and enjoyable) trips and it was interesting to see such a unique environment, even if I decided I would not go there again unless it was for business. But it made me think about the whole concept of Dubai, hence this article.

Dubai – the Land that Outsourced Itself

Dubai is seen as a centre of tourism, finance and trade, the most liberal of the Emirates. Abu Dhabi next door is more conservative, a little less cosmopolitan, but some expats prefer to live there, just as some live in Dubai and commute to Abu Dhabi. The Abu Dhabi government is seen as particularly progressive from a procurement point of view, and perhaps the leader in the region in terms of public sector procurement capability.

Fewer than 10% of Dubai residents are Emirates citizens – generally the families whose ancestors have lived in the deserts and coastal strip of the region for many, many years. The rest are 'expatriates', with the British probably the largest foreign professional-level group, and that varies from those who are working on projects only for weeks or months, to those who will see out their days in Dubai. But they cannot get citizenship, hold certain key roles in the country, and of course as Dubai is a constitutional monarchy, there is no question of participating in democratic activities.

Some observers have taken a negative view of the way the Emirates have used foreign labour, and certainly there are valid questions to be asked around the treatment of workers at the lower end of the scale, in construction and similar roles. Indeed, critics have described the situation of some Indian workers as 'indentured slavery', although we should say that these claims have been rejected strongly by those in power.

And clearly, even workers in low-paid jobs may well feel they are better off in Dubai than in rural India, Pakistan or wherever their original home may be. Indeed, at the moment, many of the folk in Dubai are VERY pleased not to be in their home countries of Syria, Libya or Egypt, given the post-Arab Spring turmoil, civil wars, and so on. And as Guy Allen suggested when we discussed this, the Maslow 'hierarchy of needs' suggests that feeling safe, a roof over our heads, and having adequate nourishment are probably more important to most of us than the right to vote.

So, it suddenly struck me that, actually, Dubai is a great outsourcing case study. The owners of the country – the ruling families – have effectively outsourced much of the operational management, development, and even some of what we might call the more strategic management of the country to millions of expats and of course the firms who employ them. Western consultants, lawyers and planners advise at the strategic level; foreign retail, property and hospitality experts and firms run the services, and foreign workers build the incredible infrastructure.

Think about it. It is all outsourced. The local Emirati people don't build the new skyscrapers that spring up almost daily. They don't tend to work in the hotels or shops or provide taxi or other services. Many of them don't even actively participate in the management-level jobs. (There is an issue there in terms of the work ethic of the younger, wealthy Emiratis, but that's for another discussion.)

Now this outsourcing might seem like a dangerous strategy. Yet, consciously or accidentally, the rulers of Dubai have put in place some very powerful mechanisms that have proved extraordinarily effective as this approach has developed. In effect, they are acting as what we would call the 'intelligent client' function in an outsourcing environment. And their strategy actually demonstrates some key elements that any organisation can mimic in terms of maintaining their own 'intelligent client' role.

The Emirati families, right up to the monarchy, consciously or accidentally, have fulfilled this role very successfully. Dubai is peaceful, stable, and, although it doesn't have the oil reserves of some other neighbouring countries, it has generally been economically successful. So, what can we learn from their example, in our more mundane outsourcing contexts?

Here are what we might call the **Dubai intelligent client rules**.

1. *Keep control of what really matters.* The state and the ruling families maintain ownership of key industries. Then there is a whole tranche of businesses where joint ventures of some sort are the norm – such as Tejari, the BravoSolution procurement technology JV. So, the intelligent client maintains a stake, but the 'suppliers' or partners have a real incentive to make it work. Then at the bottom end, suppliers (mainly individuals) get on with their activities with limited interference (and of course very low taxes). And the expats can't vote.

2. *Be willing to share gains and benefits.* As we've just said, firms and individuals have a chance to gain through their relationship. You could argue that it is easy to be generous with inherent wealth (although Dubai is not as well positioned as Saudi or Abu Dhabi in terms of oil). But clearly both firms and individuals are allowed to benefit and gain from their efforts in Dubai, some very much so.

And there are signs that even at the bottom end of the scale, workers are being treated better and seeing a fairer allocation of return for their efforts. (Some of the new 'villages' being built for factory and construction workers are apparently 'amazing' according to people who had seen them.)

3. *Strong performance management.* Sharing gains doesn't mean being soft with your service providers. I heard a couple of stories about people who were pretty unceremoniously thrown out of the country. One gets the clear impression that 'poor performance', as we might define it in supplier terms, is not tolerated. I suspect that applies at both corporate and individual level as well. Firms or people who don't work in the way the 'intelligent clients' desire don't get too many second chances – that's another pretty good learning for any outsourcing relationship.

4. *Build relationships.* Relationships are a strong part of Arabian culture of course, and that seems to apply both amongst Emiratis and with their key partners. Firms and individuals who succeed in the region do so in part because of their ability to build relationships with the key people. And even in the biggest outsourcing deal, we know that personal relationships still play an important part.

5. *Develop provider commitment to your business.* This builds on both the relationship aspect and the gain-sharing. Perhaps the comment that resonated most strongly with me during the trip came from Asif Khan, Account Director at Tejari. (He is British, with an Asian family background.) 'Many of the expats are investing in Dubai now – both emotionally and financially,' he said. 'They believe in the place, they are committed to it long-term, and they don't just see themselves as visitors.'

And that might sum up what Dubai and its rulers have achieved. They've outsourced the operations of the place to the masses of expatriates and their organisations. But they've done it in such a manner that many of the 'service providers' (as it were) are now committed to building a successful country for their own intrinsic sake, rather than purely because of what their 'contract' says they must do. (Actually, I wonder how many British citizens feel that way about building the success of our own country? How many really feel they have a stake in the UK?)

In business terms, that's a bit like a key outsourced service provider proactively helping the client find new business opportunities, or identifying cost savings, because they see their own success and future tied up so closely with that of the client firm. Now we know that we'd love that to happen more often, but it is rare to see an outsource relationship truly working like that. So, if my hypothesis is right, it's quite remarkable to see it happening in Dubai, across an entire country.

***

Back to more local issues…

The Price of Milk

The world outside our bubble doesn't take a lot of interest in procurement and supply chain issues for most of the time. But in the UK at the moment, our area has two issues on the front pages! As well as management of the Olympic security contract, now the price of milk and the complex supply chain for that product are featuring in the headlines.

More accurately, the issue is the price that farmers can get for the milk they sell from their dairy farms, and whether it is enough to provide them with a sustainable living. Much of their production goes to the big dairy processors, who convert a high proportion of it into cheese, butter, cream, yoghurt and other products, as well as selling it in liquid form to retailers and the old-fashioned door-to-door 'milkman'.

The processors, dominated by Dairy Crest (a UK publicly quoted firm), Robert Wiseman (now owned by the giant German Müller foods group) and Arla Foods (a Danish / Swedish co-operative), have reduced the price they pay to the farmers on the back of failing returns for their products, particularly cream.

Some farmers sell directly to various buyers, largely retailers, dominated by the large supermarket chains, Sainsbury's, Tesco, Asda, and so on. Interestingly, in this case, it isn't the big boys who are being most criticised by the farmers – Tesco, Sainsbury's (and Waitrose) pay a decent price. The discounters, Asda, Morrisons and, strangely, the Co-op (who trade on their image as a public-spirited organisation) were named initially as villains who wouldn't pay a reasonable price to farmers.

That caused a pretty quick response from the Co-op, who clearly can't afford their entire market positioning as good guys to be soured by this. Morrisons quickly followed, announcing they would up their payments. Others paying low prices to the farmers include large catering firms, food manufacturers – and perhaps even public sector buyers?

And the processors are also being painted as major villains, with farmers blockading processing plants. But if you look at Dairy Crest's returns and financial results over the last few years, they can hardly be accused of profiteering. Equally, if I'm a dairy buyer (and that's how I started my procurement career with Mars, many years ago), your job is to get the best value for your organisation. It would have been tough explaining to my boss that I was going to pay a few percent more than I had to in order to 'save the UK dairy industry'. It would have been my job that needed saving, I suspect.

Indeed, a Professor Andrew Cox 'power in the supply chain' analysis would be interesting for the dairy industry. It's not clear that the processors are really that powerful, although it must look like it to the farmers. But a key problem in markets like this is the unresponsiveness of supply to demand. You can't just turn off a cow; a farmer can't go on to part-time working. So relatively small changes in demand don't get the response you might expect in most other markets from the supply side.

If supply is relatively fixed, in the short to medium term, then classically price has to drop to increase demand and get the economics back into synch. But that takes us into a level of financial returns where UK farmers cannot produce milk profitably. That's partly because UK conditions are not ideal for dairy farming. They're not bad, but other countries like Ireland and New Zealand have lower costs and are better positioned on the world markets – cheaper land, more rain, more natural grass for the cows (which avoids the cost of expensive feed).

So, what happens next? Arguably, the pure market solution would be for the UK to produce less milk and allow economic activity to switch into something else. But do we really want to lose our domestic milk supply base, with potential supply continuity issues at some stage in the future? And do we want to see small dairy farms disappearing from the countryside? I suspect the farmers have done enough to get a response from the retailers that might address their complaints in the short term. But the pressures from world supply markets are likely to continue.

***

Remember the London Olympics? The first section here was written in the spring before the event.

The Dark Side of the Olympics – Hotel Price Gouging

There's been an outcry about the price of hotels in the Ukraine in particular for the 2012 European football championships. Michel Platini called them 'swindlers' over hotel prices. Reuters reported him as saying: 'You cannot raise prices from 40 euros ($52.48) to 100 euros to 500 euros from one day to the next,' added the president of European soccer's ruling body. 'That is just not done.'

Disgraceful, isn't it? Of course, hotels in the UK wouldn't do anything like that, would they?

Well ... we did a quick survey at the end of last week, looking at hotel prices for the London Olympics period. We looked at three days during the Olympics, compared to the same days of the week a month earlier, using Expedia. And we found some superb examples of opportunistic pricing.

Take a bow, the Camelot House Hotel near Paddington. Three nights – Friday to Monday – in a double or twin room in July will set you back £355.04. The same Friday to Monday stay during the Olympics? £2653.77 no less. That's over £800 a night for a 3-star hotel, awarded a mark of one out of five by Expedia users.

But they're far from the only ones. The Pacific Hotel in the same lovely area of London has rates varying from £349.04 in July up to £1577.85 in the peak Olympic period. Even the London Eye Hostel is cashing in with a rate of over £100 a night for a bed in a 14-person dormitory during the big event.

Take a bow, however, the very nice Grand Hotel off Trafalgar Square. Their rate for three nights is just £1184.40 during the Olympics, which isn't cheap, but represents a mere twice their cheapest usual rate. That seems to represent a reasonable premium, and pretty good value for what looks like a four-star-plus hotel in a great location, with good customer reviews.

I don't blame the places that are pushing their luck – goodness knows, running a small 3-star hotel in London must be a pretty soul-destroying job at the best of times. Cash in for a couple of weeks while you can. But let's not pretend we're somehow any different from the Ukrainians who are similarly taking advantage of their big sporting moment!

And advice for anyone reading this who doesn't know London too well – don't book a dodgy hotel around Paddington that gets bad TripAdvisor or Expedia user reviews. There are some real dives that aren't worth £600 a week, let alone £600 a night. Stay out of town, somewhere like Woking, that has excellent transport links into London – 25 minutes into Waterloo, so 40 minutes from Trafalgar Square (about the same as it'll take you from your hotel in Paddington or Kensington probably).

(But things had changed by July!)

You may remember back in April we featured the prices certain hotels were hoping to charge during the Olympics. Well, we heard at the weekend that tourist-related businesses in London are beginning to panic in terms of bookings both during the event and for the rest of the summer (the British weather can't be helping either). That includes hotels, restaurants and West End shows.

So, we thought we'd go back and take a look at the hotels we featured in April and see how their prices on Expedia compare now.

Firstly, we have the Camelot House Hotel near Paddington, which in April was quoting no less than £2653.77 for three nights in a double room over the middle Olympic weekend. Now? You can have a triple room for just £630.

Then we have the Pacific Hotel in the same part of London. In April, they were looking for a mere £1577.85 for three nights. Now they'll do you a double room for £525 for the same Friday – Monday period.

We reserved our praise last time for The Grand, off Trafalgar Square, who were charging a not too ridiculous £1184.40 (given it is a much higher rates hotel than the others featured here). And even their rate has seen a significant reduction, to £920 for three nights.

So, while maybe they are still not exactly bargains, it now looks like if you still need a room in London during the Olympics, you don't have to get ripped off too badly. Mind you, if you paid £2000+ when you booked ahead, you may be feeling somewhat sick now.

Looking at prices for later in August, post the event, there are some real bargains emerging, which supports the report of poor forward bookings. Have a look at the 'Top Secret' hotel sites, and you can get a very good four-star Central London hotel for around £100 midweek in August – a rare event indeed.

One other point from all this. The whole hotel market has changed completely in terms of pricing strategy since the growth of the Internet. It's now – as we can see from this analysis – a market with quite incredible price volatility, as rates change in a real-time response to fluctuations in supply and demand. Much like oil, cocoa, or gold really – but arguably even more volatile.

So, with our procurement hat on, we can ask if major travel buyers have responded to this, because we know that commodity markets require different strategies to other markets? Are the most innovative travel buyers using new approaches – or is it still a case of locking up deals based on a guaranteed number of room nights agreement (as I used to do many years ago in this market)?

I don't know the answer to that – it's quite a few years since I bought travel – but I'd be interested to hear from any buyers who are taking advantage of this change in the dynamics of the market.

***

And finally, for this chapter, I show that almost anything can be turned into a discussion about some aspect of procurement management!

SPOTY Gets the Evaluation Process Wrong

Tender and bid evaluation can be a pretty dry subject, but, procurement and statistics geek that I am at heart, I am fascinated by the 'numbers' element of evaluating bids and tenders. It's also a very important subject, although often not considered fully or properly by senior people. How you choose the best supplier is, when you come down to it, a pretty key part of procurement's role.

For instance, how you 'score' price is a bit of a specialist subject of mine, and simply this factor (and I don't mean the weighting you give to price, I mean how you actually convert price to a score for purposes of the evaluation) can make a huge difference to who wins a tender.

So today we'll illustrate a particular aspect of the process with reference to the recent furore the BBC have faced over their choosing of the shortlist for the UK's Sports Personality of the Year (SPOTY). The fuss is over the fact that the shortlist of 10 does not include a single woman.

How could this happen? Potential female candidates included world-class or world champion athletes, swimmers, and arguably the toughest woman in the sports world – Chrissie Wellington, 4-times world 'Ironman' (triathlon) champion.

The problem was with the voting system, and the first issue was around the people who made the decision about the composition of the shortlist. 27 sports writers were asked to nominate 10 people each. They included representatives of those fine sporting publications Nuts and Zoo; many have described them as simply softcore porn mags. As sportswoman rarely perform topless, that may have put potential female candidates at a possible disadvantage with those magazines, and neither named a woman on their list. (Mind you, neither did *The Independent* or the *Evening Standard*.)

Then we had the *Manchester Evening News*, who nominated four Manchester-based footballers, none of whom seemed to have done anything particularly special this year, including Dimitar Berbatov, Sir Alex Ferguson's 6th choice striker currently … Oh yes, and two Lancashire cricketers!

So, the first lesson – make sure your evaluators are people with credibility in your organisation, who understand what they are assessing. How were these 27 selected? Was any attempt made to balance them in terms of sporting preferences, locality, gender, experience? Was there any sort of qualification process for the evaluators? Did they have any guidelines from the BBC in terms of what they were looking for (the selection criteria, in procurement terms) in the nominees? At the very least, you would have thought they should have been encouraged not to let stupidly parochial factors creep into their selection.

We then saw the problem of *averaging* come into play. The votes from the 27 judges were added up, and the top 10 scores made up the shortlist. This had the advantage of getting rid of Berbatov and similar outliers, but it introduced a new problem – that of the averaging effect.

We have often similar problems with bid evaluation. If the marks from individual evaluators are simply averaged, we might see one evaluator who thinks a bid, or a particular response, is worth 9/10. The other evaluator makes it 1/10, so we have an average of 5/10.

Now the one thing we can say with some certainty is that 5/10 is not the 'correct' score for the bid! It looks like it is either great – or rubbish. There has been some very different interpretation by the two evaluators, or an error. We need to find out what the issue is and arrive at the 'correct' score for the bid. So, *consensus scoring* is the answer to this and most of the other problems identified here.

Imagine if this group of markers for SPOTY had got together. The four Manchester footballers would have been laughed out of the running immediately. Then someone would have mentioned Chrissie Wellington – 4-times world champion Ironman Triathlon and the toughest female sportswoman in the world. I'm pretty sure others who maybe didn't know of her would have said, 'Wow! Of course, she should be on the list!' The absence of women would also have been noted and perhaps addressed.

And that brings us into a tricky area in terms of evaluation, for the public sector in particular. Let's say that you want to take five suppliers through to tender from a pre-qualification process. *Brilliant Inc* is the top scorer. In 5th place comes *Boring plc* – well behind Brilliant, and they are very much the same type of firm, with a similar approach, profile, style – they're just not as good. But in your PQQ they just outscored *Maverick Ltd*, who are a very different firm, with some weaknesses, but would offer a very different option at tender stage to Brilliant Inc.

Who do you select? I would suggest the best thing for the organisation is to take Maverick Ltd through to tender rather than Boring plc. Boring stand little or no chance of winning the work, as they are a pale imitation of Brilliant. Whereas Maverick might just come through, and at least by offering a different approach they may inform the bidding process in a positive manner.

We have the same parallel with SPOTY. No offence to him, as he seems like an excellent chap, but Luke Donald cannot win. He's up against two other golfers, both Major winners – McIlroy who has the youth thing going for him, and Darren Clarke, Open Champion at 42 after 20 years of trying, who has the backstory and huge popular support. If a golfer wins, it just isn't going to be Donald. Sorry, Luke. So why waste a shortlist place on him? Because of the daft evaluation system.

This is tricky in the public sector where the number 5 in the scoring trumps the number 6. But you can try and ask questions to give the opportunity for some originality to come through even at PQQ stage. And when you come to the borderline cases, there may be a little flexibility and the consensus discussion can explore that. In the private sector, where one is less constrained, look to get a balanced, varied tender list, not necessarily just the top five suppliers based on raw scores.

And SPOTY? Mark Cavendish is my prediction. (*And yes, I was correct!)*

***

Chapter 4

THE PUBLIC SECTOR

The UK public sector spends something comfortably over £200 billion a year with suppliers of one sort or another. Globally, public procurement is a multi-trillion-dollar business, with estimates suggesting it is around 20% of all global GDP.

It is also very much in the public eye, for obvious reasons. Much of what is bought affects the lives of many citizens. Issues such as corruption come to the fore in some countries, and on a positive note (for us writers anyway), a lot more gets into the public domain than, say, news about how Ford, Shell or Amazon conduct their procurement.

So, there are always good stories for me to talk about, often with some sort of wider public interest. Even if you don't work in the public sector, I'd hope there is plenty for you to enjoy here in this section.

Let's start with Tesco. A few years back, there was a lot of noise around in terms of how public sector procurement 'should be more like Tesco'. This was before Tesco was hit with a big accounting scandal and various accusations suggesting that the way they worked with suppliers was, let's say, not exactly best practice. We didn't hear much more of the comparison after all that, but actually the argument is still an interesting one. Basically, while I am the first to be critical of public procurement when done badly, it is a very complex environment.

Procurement at Tesco – It's Nothing Like Government

A paper titled 'Towards Tesco – improving public sector procurement', supported by the Institute of Directors, was published recently. Here are four reasons (there are more) why the public sector is NOT like Tesco.

Mission

Tesco's mission is to make profit for its shareholders. I'm one of them, have been for 20 years, and they've done a great job for me. One of my better buys. They do not have to worry about caring for the sick or disadvantaged, providing a basic standard of living for the citizen, generating national economic wealth (and happiness?), protecting the nation, providing educational and health services, or keeping our persons and property save from wrongdoers.

They have no wider responsibilities to their suppliers other than what maximises long-term shareholder value, and that is how it should be. It seems obvious that this fundamental contrast leads to some major differences in how procurement has to be undertaken by the public sector compared to Tesco.

Uniformity

Tesco runs lots of shops. Some are big, some are small. But they are basically all the same. They can all use the same suppliers for many goods and services, and indeed the same specifications. There is one set of IT systems because there is one set of shops.

Contrast that even with a single small local authority (council), which on its own is a more complex 'business' in terms of what it does, by a significant factor, than Tesco's entire organisation. A council runs what are effectively businesses in leisure, in retail, in care services, in transport ... It also buys everything from tree surgery to taxi services, from books to foster care services.

Now that's just councils. When we look at the commonalty or standardisation across different parts of the public sector, the comparison with Tesco breaks down even further. We've also got police forces, hospitals, schools, central Departments, universities ... what is the commonality between a school in rural Northumberland, a large hospital in London, the British Waterways Board, the SAS (military heroes) and Devon Police? How standardised are their requirements and how much commonality is there across that supply base?

Control

Ultimately, Philip Clarke (Tesco CEO) can sack a store manager who says, 'I want to buy my own deep freezers and energy for my store.' Of course, the whole idea is crazy because of the very standardisation we've discussed. Francis Maude or even David Cameron cannot fire:

- A Foundation Trust (hospital etc.) Chief Executive
- A Police Commissioner or even Chief Constable
- A Council Leader or Council Chief Executive
- A headmaster

They even struggle to fire senior civil servants, as we're seeing in the case of Transport and the West Coast Railways incident. There's no central power that can demand compliance, there is no mandate. And in fact, these public bodies are increasingly competitors as the coalition government tries to encourage that between hospitals, schools. So apart from anything else, the report's ideas run counter to the whole political philosophy of this age.

Size

We tend to think Tesco is big, but it pales into insignificance compared to the public sector. Tesco probably spends a few million in legal fees or consulting, maybe even into the tens of millions. The public sector spends billions just on professional services. Tesco's IT spend? Less than HMRC or DWP, I'd bet, who are themselves just a fraction of total public sector spend. Another invalid comparator.

So repeat after me. The public sector is not 'just like Tesco', never will be and shouldn't be. That's not to say public procurement can't learn something from the best in the private sector. Of course it can. But the comparison is facile and immediately sets us off on that illogical and ill-founded route that leads to the crazy 'centralise all public procurement' argument.

***

UK local authorities (county, city and town councils) have been through a phase of seeing outsourcing of services as a panacea. We suspect the tide has turned, but there have been some real failures along the way.

Local Authorities and Ill-Judged Outsourcing

Local authorities seem to be hurtling towards ill-judged outsourcing in a desperate attempt to balance the books.

Senior executives I suspect see this as a bit of a no-lose situation. If they end up working for BT, Serco or whoever, they'll probably make more money than they do as public servants. If they don't transfer, they'll get generous pay-offs. (Interesting to see that Katherine Kerswell has become Director-General for Civil Service Reform in the Cabinet Office. She picked up a £420,000 pay-off last year when, as Chief Executive for Kent County Council, she fell out with Paul Carter, the Council leader.)

Councillors themselves – well, how many of them have run a procurement process or managed a contract worth several hundred million pounds? They seem to be easily seduced by fine words from the supply side – at heart, I suspect it is simply that they have no idea themselves how they would reduce costs by the 20%+ they need to, so they respond enthusiastically to those who claim that they do have the answer.

The latest example is Cornwall County Council, where, in a triumph for democracy, the 'Cabinet' of councillors has decided to go ahead with an outsourcing process despite the full council body voting 45-28 against it! I do find that extraordinary. Just think if that had happened in the Middle East or China – the UK media would be shaking their heads about sham democracy and oligarchy. But it happens in Cornwall, and no one seems to care too much.

So, they're proceeding with an outsource, with BT and CSC as the two shortlisted firms. (I'll give you a strong prediction as to who is going to win that fight…) But yet again, the worrying thing is that procurement is lumped into the list of requirements as an apparent afterthought, as we've seen in North Tyneside and elsewhere. This fundamentally looks like an IT outsource, but procurement and commissioning get thrown into the pot.

And if you outsource procurement, who is going to manage CSC / BT?

There's also the classic Southwest One / London Metropolitan University fallacy – that if we set up some 'public / private partnership', then lots of other public bodies will come on-board and join our venture, making lots of money for the original partners.

IT WON'T HAPPEN. I KEEP TELLING YOU.

No one will join your venture, because even if you do eventually get it right, it will take you years to establish your own outsourcing as a success. No one will join until that is very evident. Other public bodies will follow their own path in the meantime. And there's every chance your venture will fail – better than evens, I would say, looking at the track record so far in local government.

And I do hope that the people of Cornwall identify those Cabinet members who seem to think democracy doesn't apply to them, and 'throw the scoundrels out' at the next election. (Google has failed me as to the source of that quote, incidentally.)

(Note – I was right to be sceptical, the Cornwall deal with BT lasted just two years but cost the council and residents a small fortune.)

***

Outsourcing – Points for Councillors to Note

The UK's local authorities (councils), police forces and other public bodies are showing an unprecedented interest in outsourcing. There have been high-profile outsourcing decisions or events in councils including Somerset, Cornwall, Barnet and elsewhere, with the interest certain to continue as councils struggle to maintain services in the light of funding shortfalls.

Over the holiday period, the Chief Executive of Cornwall, Kevin Lavery, announced he was leaving, just as their councillors have to make a tricky decision about outsourcing – this follows a period during which he was a strong advocate of a very significant, widescale outsourcing / partnership with BT.

Councillors themselves have to make difficult decisions without always having the right skills or very good information to support the decision. Some individuals no doubt have relevant experience, but for others, complex issues and decisions around outsourcing must take them well outside their areas of experience, knowledge and comfort. We really don't envy them.

And we're not against outsourcing in any sense here; every organisation outsources something, and it is a vital tool for pretty much any and every organisation today. But for people in a governance or decision-making role in public bodies, or with the ability to influence decisions, we'd suggest they should consider these four contextual points.

1. Remember that your potential and actual suppliers are inevitably motivated by short- and long-term profit motives at both corporate and individual level. Nothing wrong with that, but never forget it. The sales people you deal with may be heavily incentivised, and their bonus for closing the deal may be more than your staff earn in a year. Respect their views, but never forget what motivates them and their firms. Whatever they tell you, they are not your 'friends', and whilst they generally do want you to succeed, that is because it will best serve their own interests.

2. Remember that the executives within your organisation, who may be promoting a current outsourcing initiative, may not be around to see it up and running (as in the case of Mr Lavery). They may have great loyalty to your organisation and plan to see out their careers with you – or they might not. They may not even be here next year or next month. Respect their views but remember they have their own interests, may go their own way, and might leave whatever they have promoted or created to someone else to implement or rescue.

3. Remember that you may also not be around in a few years' time. Wanting to leave a legacy is understandable. But realise that someone else may have to pick up the pieces if you make mistakes now. That shouldn't mean your decision-making can be cavalier; think about how you want your actions and decisions to be remembered in the future, and how you want your successors to talk about you when you're no longer around.

4. Remember that the financial situation of your organisation may be very different in the future. There is no guarantee that income is going to grow again in real terms – perhaps ever. Service requirements and priorities will also inevitably change. So, any significant contractual arrangements you enter should be flexible enough to cope with this. Don't get locked into unaffordable costs or inflexible service definitions.

And good luck.

***

While we're talking about poor practice, my major feat of proper investigative journalism was probably exposing the Ministry of Defence contract with consulting firm AlixPartners. It was agreed without proper competitive processes and involved eye-wateringly high daily rates for the consultants. It got covered eventually in The Times, *Private Eye and elsewhere, but it all started actually with an anonymous phone call to me! I wrote a lot about it, so here are just some highlights.*

AlixPartners and MOD

We've learnt that the MOD awarded a contract to the US consulting firm AlixPartners to assist the MOD with a 'period of intense negotiation with a number of our major industrial suppliers'.

The work was not advertised, and no other firms were asked to bid for the work, which could be worth up to £12 million for AlixPartners over the next year or so. 'Very tight timescales' was quoted as the reason for the lack of competition.

AlixPartners are not as far as we know on any existing UK Government framework contract and they're not a firm who have a high profile (in my experience) in Government circles; but they seem to have around 100 UK-based staff, and, having looked at their website, clearly have some impressive people. Anyway, someone in MOD likes them enough to engage them in this direct manner.

(Some months later…)

We have featured our investigation into the UK Ministry of Defence's consulting contract with AlixPartners several times – we got the contract finally through an FOI (Freedom of Information) request, but the consultant day rate was 'redacted', i.e. kept secret. We complained about this, and last week we had a nice letter from the MOD's Head of Corporate Information, Katie de Bourcier, saying that 'the arguments for disclosure outweigh those in favour of release'. Thank you, Katie.

So, we have what is virtually the whole contract now. The names of the consultants cannot be released – which is fine, we don't give a damn frankly who they are. But we do care about the rates, which are now public. The contract lists two Managing Directors and six Directors of AlixPartners who have been engaged by MOD, all at the same day rate, which is £3950.

They are contracted for between 132 and 396 days each, giving 2,354 days in total and a total cost of £9,298,300. Plus, we have the 30% 'success fee' on top of this, which takes those rates up to £5,135 per day, plus VAT, which makes it £6,162 a day. Then we have expenses, such as mileage and the consultants' lunch allowance of £10. No, really, they can claim that on top of the six grand a day! And Alix can have a rate increase during the contract, too – inflation adjusting as it were. (It seems pretty clear who drafted the contract.)

OK, let's take out VAT, as at least that stays within the public purse. But that's still over £5,000. Per person. Per day.

Now, even if this contract had been awarded through a full and open competition, we would have severe doubts. But this was awarded, in our opinion, illegally in terms of EU regulations – without open competition or a full procurement process. We've found no evidence of any fraud or corruption in the process, we should stress.

However great a job AlixPartners is doing – ironically, their role is to help MOD negotiate with suppliers to get better deals – this level of fees is ridiculous and way above market prices, we would suggest. And all at a time when the Forces are struggling to meet the demands of several wars, and a recent announcement outlined that a further 7,000 MOD civilian jobs would go. We don't really go for hyperbole here, so we use the word with some hesitation, but these rates are obscene, and the lack of proper competition is disgraceful.

We wrote to Ursula Brennan, the Permanent Secretary at MOD, a month ago, asking her to cancel the contract – we're still waiting for a reply to that. We'll let you know. But we did get a comment from the Efficiency and Reform Group in Cabinet Office.

'For some reason this contract between MOD and AlixPartners fell outside of the normal Cabinet Office – ERG approvals process, where all such consultancy engagements, likely to be over nine months in duration, require Minister for the Cabinet Office and Chief Procurement Officer review and approval. Given the time frames, MOD Commercial colleagues will be asked to present their case from a value for money perspective over the next few weeks.'

Interesting – do you get the feeling Cabinet Office are not very happy with MOD? They have known about this for months, so getting MOD to present their case 'over the next few weeks' is hardly a rapid response. And here is the MOD press office comment:

'AlixPartners is providing specialist assistance in negotiations with industrial suppliers to deliver significant savings across defence within very tight timescales and overall is expected to save hundreds of millions of pounds. Overall the MOD has delivered dramatic savings to its consultancy expenditure and it is now a tenth of what it was five years ago.'

(Later still …)

We now have the final instalment (probably) from this sad tale. And it's a case of the good, the bad and the ugly … The good is that MOD terminated the contract early, before the full potential £12 million was spent.

'I can confirm that because the activities under the Alix contract have now successfully delivered, with the last piece of work just concluding, we have exercised the break clause in the contract and the contract will cease on 23rd December (per its normal notice period).'

The bad is that not only have MOD still spent £7.59m, but they also do appear to have paid the 30% success fee. Following a Freedom of Information request, we've been told this: 'The total amount paid to AlixPartners for consultancy services under the contract was £7.59m (VAT exc), of which £1.75m (VAT exc) related to the success fee provisions of the contract'.

So, I make that £5.84M pre-bonus plus 30% which is £7.59m.

Now I do know that some MOD staff were keen not to pay the full bonus – they felt as strongly as we did that the rates were pretty generous already at £3950 per person-day. But I suspect the contract was worded in a manner that made it tough for MOD to get out of that.

And finally, the ugly. No one has taken any accountability for this example of what is, at best, very poor procurement practice. We could ask the EU to look into the inappropriate lack of open competition, and eventually there could be a rap on the knuckles of the MOD and the UK. But that seems a little pointless in the greater scheme of things. It's also clear that the guys at the top of MOD procurement now had little or nothing to do with this whole episode.

So, we're not going to pursue it further, but (not wishing to sound too sanctimonious here), let's just hope that we've played a small part in encouraging others in public procurement not to bend or break the rules, and pay way over the odds, in the interests of expediency.

***

Another campaigning post, and a cause that others are still continuing to pursue. Eventually we might get there …

Corruption, Transparency, Suppliers and FOI

We've featured a couple of posts this week with a similar theme. Firstly, our 'Yes Minister' homage, with Sir Humphrey explaining how a favourite consultant can be engaged without anything as tricky as a procurement process. Then a slightly darker tale of corruption disguised by use of a prime contractor, again avoiding competition and public scrutiny.

Our point was to illustrate a loophole that might seem like a trivial matter but is a major danger to the integrity of our public services. Prime contractors to the public sector have total freedom in terms of how they place work with subcontractors: not only do they not have to follow any set procurement process, but also their activities have limited visibility to the outside world.

And 'Primes', as we've reported before, are doing more and more work that once would have been the preserve of the public sector itself. This is driving opportunity for corruption and fraud – and making it harder for the public to assess competence and value for money as well in some cases.

Even before the Freedom of Information regulations came into force, you could usually, if you tried hard enough, find out whether proper procurement processes had been followed in public sector bodies. As the last resort, a legal challenge would get to the bottom of (for instance) how bidders for a certain contract had been evaluated and why a certain firm had been chosen.

But if we're trying to examine why and how a Prime contractor (appointed properly themselves, let's assume), chose their subcontractors, we're potentially in the dark. They may have done so through totally professional and effective means. Or corruption might have seeped into their organisation and influenced the decision; or as in our theoretical examples, the public sector organisation might have exerted pressure on the Prime for motives that weren't totally pure.

That might be the fairly harmless Sir Humphrey example – oiling the wheels to make things happen, getting things done that probably are the 'right' things to do. Or it could be the corrupt public servant getting kickbacks or pushing the business via the Prime to favoured suppliers for personal gain.

There are other examples where the lack of transparency of what goes on in the supply chain is worrying as contractors carry out more and more sensitive work (in the police and security sector, for the Work Programme, with the armed forces). Are those contractors bound by the same codes of conduct on whistleblowing, for instance? Do they have the same constraints on their actions or accountability to the public?

Now, you might argue that all of this can be handled by good contracting and contract management. And to some extent that is true. The public authority can request for instance that the Prime responds positively to FOI. But I think we need to go further. We need a binding code of conduct for contractors that covers these issues and probably some new legislation, including making contractors to the public sector subject to FOI when that question relates to their work for the public sector.

Contractors would resist this like mad – and there is a cost involved of course. But actually, I'm in favour of tightening up somewhat the rules of FOI to stop frivolous requests, which would mitigate the cost element. And ultimately, this would be a very small burden for the good suppliers who have nothing to hide and already have decent processes which drive good value and guard against corruption.

I'm not conceptually opposed to outsourcing of public sector work, but if we want it to be done effectively and honestly, we need some more governance around some of these issues. Otherwise I'm concerned that the next wave of scandals will be around these issues. That might come from within the Primes and their supply chains – or it may come from public sector buyers / commissioners working together with suppliers against the best interests of the public and taxpayers. Because one thing we do know is that if there are easy ways for fraud and corruption to blossom, it will.

***

After some negative stories so far in this section, let's look at a good news story! The BBC has had a very strong procurement function for years now, and despite all the criticism it gets from some quarters, it is one of the very best organisations in the country in many ways.

Digital Switchover – What Went Wrong? (Answer – Nothing)

With all the gloomy stories about public sector procurement, and the troubles at the BBC, let's celebrate a real public sector (sort of) procurement success story with a BBC angle – the switch to digital TV. Here's digital spy website:

'Britain has today bid farewell to more than 70 years of analogue television, after the final stage of the £630 million digital switchover project was completed in Northern Ireland.'

You didn't really notice, did you? Clearly, it all went very smoothly.

Well, if you go back to the announcement of the change, that wasn't the prognosis. There were regular press stories about how it was all going to be a disaster – in particular, how the old, infirm or marginalised would find themselves without TV post-switchover, sitting helplessly in front of their blank analogue screens. This was a typical report.

> The elderly are in danger of being left in the dark about the switch to digital TV. Those who need help most are not getting information and technical support, says a report for regulator Ofcom.

So, the BBC and Digital UK put in place the Digital Switchover Help Scheme, delivered via a third-party contract, to provide support to those who needed it – 'vulnerable people' in some sense – in terms of helping them make the change. (I'll declare an interest here, as I had some limited governance-level involvement with the procurement process in the early days.)

It was a fascinating service requirement and therefore procurement. The services included call centre, various communications approaches, staff to actually go into homes and install aerials, financial management … it was a very complex service, with all sorts of sensitivities. (How do you deal with and explain options to an elderly, disabled lady living alone who doesn't speak English?)

An added complication was the need to run a pilot, for which a contract had to be let quickly, without prejudicing the market for the main tender. Capita duly won the competition for the pilot, to no one's surprise, but then lost out to Eaga (since acquired by Carillion) in the main tender, which was a surprise. But it was a demonstration of a skilful procurement process which managed to maintain real competition through the pilot phase and right up to the final decision.

The risk transfer issues were also challenging. No one knew quite how much work would be needed. So how much risk should the supplier hold? A complete fixed price deal would have been possible, but it was decided that the BBC was better placed to manage most of the volume risk – however, a lot of operational risk was transferred to the provider.

So, several years on, what was the outcome?

Well, the switch-over is complete. I have not found one single press report of 'old folks left with no TV'. Or 'workmen who claimed to be installing an aerial for me trashed my house and stole my life savings'. Or 'my new TV exploded after rogue workmen installed a new aerial'. These were typical concerns back in the early days of the scheme.

And the decisions on risk transfer were totally vindicated. It's actually a good story – the experience showed that more people than estimated were either capable of doing things themselves or had friends and family who would rally round and help.

So, usage of the scheme was well below plan, and the total cost has come in at £260m against the budget of £603m – £343m has been returned to the government.

From my limited role early on, I can honestly say the BBC procurement and project team involved was first-class, and the top people at the BBC extremely impressive. When George Entwistle got the top job in the BBC recently, I thought, 'Good gracious, he must be good if he's beaten Caroline Thomson to it,' because she (the COO then) and Zarin Patel (the CFO) were two of the most impressive people I've met in my business career.

It's good to see a very satisfactory outcome to the programme anyway – and just a shame that good news doesn't get as much attention as bad.

***

There is also a load of nonsense talked about public sector procurement. The argument that 'the private sector should not gain from education' (or health, or whatever) is one of the common ones we hear.

Public Procurement, Private Gain?

We featured recently the challenges facing DWP (the UK government's Department for Work & Pensions) and their procurement team given the issues around the Work Programme, designed to help get people into jobs.

Recent claims that this was in effect free labour for large firms, helping them to increase profits and maybe even reducing their need for paid workers, have led to some outcry and a number of firms pulling out of the government scheme.

That was then linked to the fraud investigations going on around A4e, one of the leading providers of employment services. The A4e Chair, and one of the founders of the firm, Emma Harrison, first stood down as Prime Minister David Cameron's adviser on problem families, then resigned from her A4e role.

That led to comments in the media about the philosophical and moral issue of private firms benefiting from this sort of activity – helping people into jobs. Some saw it as 'immoral' that firms were receiving state funding and making a profit out of the unemployed. We've seen the same in Education, where even the economically bone-dry Tory Michael Gove has had to tread gently around the issue of firms potentially making money out of running state schools.

And yet, think of all the firms that make money out of health and the National Health Service. I don't mean simply private hospitals doing NHS work, but (most fundamentally perhaps) what about drugs companies? They make huge profits. Should they all be charities, or not-for-profit organisations of some sort? (Making money out of dying babies? How dare they!?)

Then there are firms making money and receiving cash from the state for taking our rubbish away or providing care for old folks. Are those any less worthy causes than support to jobseekers? So why don't we get hung up on those services being provided by private firms? And what about food and water? Perhaps even more basic to human existence than health or education or work. How can we tolerate firms making profit out of these essentials?

It seems very illogical that we get worked up about some of these things and not others. Personally, I have no philosophical issues with the private sector delivering anything on behalf of the government, as it were. But it all comes down to good procurement. (There, you knew we'd get back to procurement eventually!)

Because if we are going to have private providers involved in sensitive areas, then, in order for the process to succeed, someone has to ensure that certain things happen, and the taxpayer needs to see that those things are happening to have faith in the process.

The competitive process must be transparent and fair; there must be strong barriers against fraud and corruption; contracts must be carefully constructed with aligned objectives, fair returns for success and penalties for failure; there need to be measures to protect against excessive profits; and contract / supplier management needs to ensure transparency, proper delivery against the contract, and propriety at all times.

If all this can be achieved, then I have no problem with private sector delivery of services on behalf of government.

That's also why, despite all the frustrations, I'm personally still fascinated by complex public procurement issues and challenges – they have an impact on everyone in ways you rarely see in the private sector. And the complexity, scope and volume of these challenges are only likely to increase if we see more private sector firms as providers in these complex areas.

Despite the current furore around the employment issue, it seems more than likely that this will be the case, leading to even more focus on the strength and depth of public procurement capability. No pressure, ladies and gentlemen of public procurement!

***

Over the last 15 years or so, we've seen a huge growth in people talking about 'commissioning' of services in a public sector context. But is commissioning really different from 'procurement'? And if so, why? They are the questions I tried to answer here.

Procurement and Commissioning – What's the Difference?

'Commissioning', and how it relates to 'procurement', has become important in a number of sectors, perhaps most so in health (e.g. commissioning of health services from hospitals) and local government (social care, children's services etc.).

I want to explore what commissioning is and look in some detail at why it is positioned as something different from procurement. If we don't even have clarity around what commissioning really is, if key stakeholders don't understand how it relates to procurement in terms of processes, skills required and so on, then it's hard to see that we're likely to see great performance.

But let's start by looking at procurement. There are three broad key stages to what we'd call the strategic sourcing / procurement cycle – and note we're not talking about the transactional or P2P process here.

Stage 1 – Identify and understand the requirements / specifications, and analyse the market to establish whether it can meet the requirements. If necessary, carry out market-making activities. Consider the market and requirements in order to develop the most appropriate sourcing strategy.

Stage 2 – Select the supplier(s). That may or may not involve a competitive process, such as a formal tendering exercise, and / or negotiation. It also involves development of a formal contract in most cases.

Stage 3 – Manage the contract and the supplier to ensure they deliver against the contract, and that risks and opportunities are managed, including changes in requirements through the contract period.

Now, when we read documents describing commissioning, the process would appear to fit this model perfectly. In an area like health, there is rightly a lot of emphasis on understanding the needs of the recipients of medical services, and of matching this to what is available in the market or creating new supply options if they are needed. That's our stage 1, so no real difference between procurement and commissioning there.

Another possible differentiation is that commissioning involves 'designing' the service. That's something I've heard from local authorities – but the cynic in me says this is what you and I might call 'writing the specification'. But even if it is more than that, it is not fundamentally too far from the procurement development task of (for example) looking for a supplier to handle a tricky IT outsource or a complex global marketing assignment. The same basics of understanding the needs and the market, and aligning the two, remain.

And even where there is some genuine creativity involved, that will usually be an iteration between what is wanted and what is available in the market – something buyers of complex services or products have done for years. Twenty-five years ago, when in the private sector I looked for firms who could manufacture Easter eggs for my firm, there wasn't a ready supply market in place, and we had to 'design the service'.

Equally, post-contract management in a 'commissioning' environment stresses the need to monitor and measure supplier performance, manage improvement, and meet changing needs. Just as we would with our facilities management provider or a supplier of key auto parts in that industry.

So, despite the claims that commissioning is very different from procurement, the actual core processes do not support that argument. We therefore conclude that the fundamental processes of procurement and commissioning are very similar.

But is commissioning different because of what is being bought? Well, we're getting a bit closer, but it still doesn't quite work. It clearly isn't just health these days – commissioning is being used to describe procurement of everything from building maintenance services, through waste management to marketing projects and social care. Many of these categories are bought in the private sector as well as public, and we don't hear private firms talking about commissioning their repairs and maintenance contracts.

The most distinctive element of commissioning is that, unlike most traditional procurement, the goods or (usually) services bought are often provided to recipients who are *external* to the organisation that both funds the purchase and runs the procurement process.

On the other hand, in the case of traditional procurement, the purchased items are consumed by the buying firm – in their factories (raw materials, packaging, components), by their own staff (fleet, stationery, laptops), or to support their own activities (marketing, professional or IT services, plant maintenance).

Now, if that is the main difference, we can see why it needs some different emphasis and activities, and maybe even skills, compared to 'traditional' procurement. Understanding the needs and requirements of a few hundred thousand citizens (patients) in a medical commissioning area is not the same as determining what capabilities the sales force need for their mobile phones.

Interestingly, the point at which commissioning is covering services for which the recipient will pay fully, like elements of social care provision, we have moved into the territory of another major subset of 'procurement' – that of what is usually called retail buying or 'goods for resale', for supermarkets and many other types of retailer.

Finally, we might ask just why commissioning has become seen as something so different from procurement? How about:

1. The failure of public sector procurement to demonstrate that it was interested in and competent at the full cycle of what we define as the procurement process. Too many public procurement staff and organisations were focused almost solely on that middle part of the process, ignoring both market development and contract management.

2. Some realisation that there is a genuine difference (see above) and the implications for how procurement needs to be undertaken where we have that 'external recipient' situation.

3. A positive desire to define a new profession in the public sector, one that would be taken seriously (quite rightly), and be seen as more prestigious than conventional procurement, which (very unfortunately for us in the profession) had become too associated with tactical and transactional buying in too many organisations.

4. The less positive side of that point – as some of our commentators have said, simply 'people who didn't want to be called procurement people'.

But if the commissioning 'profession' sees itself as divorced from the procurement profession, both will miss out because, as I hope we've shown, the commonality is far more significant than the differences.

***

Of all the terrible stories of recent years, one of the most shocking was around grooming and abuse of teenage girls by groups of men in various UK cities and towns such as Rotherham. This exposed issues around how 'difficult' children are handled in this country and even threw up some procurement angles. I was genuinely furious about the lack of interest in procurement relating to children in care, while Ministers seemed obsessed with harmonising the price of stationery across government departments!

Rochdale Kids in Care – Exploited in Different Ways

Sometimes stories are just so awful it's hard to know where to start, or even whether to try. The recent news about the convictions of groups of men for abusing young girls was just one such case. Yet it raised some procurement issues that seemed worth airing further.

The Times discovered that one of the teenage girls involved had been the *only* resident of a care home – I had no idea these 'solo care' homes existed. She was from Essex originally, but was placed in the Green Corns home in Rochdale in 2009, aged 14. Rochdale Council contracted for this home, with an annual contract value of £252,000.

That paid for six staff who supposedly provided around-the-clock care for the girl – except of course it wasn't 'care', as we would expect it, or around the clock, because they seemed unable to stop her wandering off and getting involved in drugs, sex, prostitution and abuse.

So apart from all the other horrendous aspects of this case, was this a procurement failure? It certainly looks that way. It's very hard to see that the service as purchased / commissioned was fit for purpose, offered good value for money, or delivered the outcomes required.

The Times had other interesting facts, including that this and other similar solo care homes had been bought and sold several times. For instance:

> In 2004 Green Corns, by now operating 30 homes in north-west England, was sold for £26 million to a group headed by 3i, the private equity company.

Now £26m is way over the underlying property value and suggests that the market valued each of these 30 homes at around £900k. That in turn suggests that the buyer saw a reliable profit stream of approaching £100,000 after tax per home, I suspect, looking at the returns a private equity buyer might expect.

That would fit with a business model that says, for a single home, we charge £250k, pay perhaps £120k in salaries, perhaps £30k for food and other running costs – and there's still enough left to cover the capital costs and leave a nice profit.

Reports looking at this home talked about staff without the right skills and training, so one assumes that these weren't people paid particularly high wages. From *The Times* again:

> Ofsted has responsibility for inspecting children's homes. Records of its twice-yearly visits to the Rochdale home – one of 18 Green Corns solo homes in the town – reveal that staff did not even meet the very basic minimum qualification required for residential childcare. They also show that care workers had no training in the needs of a child at risk of sexual exploitation.

So, we can question a number of aspects with our procurement hats on.

- Did the commissioners understand the full cost model of the provider, how much was spent on staff, profit levels? And did they feel these were appropriate?
- How was the requirement and the service defined?
- Were there any performance metrics for the provider, any links between performance and payment or any attempt to link payment to outcomes?
- How was contract management executed? – after those Ofsted reports, why didn't the Council act?

We're not particularly singling out Rochdale for criticism here. This was a desperate case, with what sounds like virtually uncontrollable young people, who presumably couldn't be put in a fostering situation. So, we should have sympathy with the commissioners, as well as the kids in question and indeed the staff, carrying out a virtually impossible job.

But this can't be right. Spending over £250,000 a year of taxpayers' money – in a pretty depressed area – to look after one girl, and to fail so comprehensively to deliver even the most basic level of care. £250,000, and the child was drugged and raped by gangs of middle-aged men.

And this is where I could get quite annoyed about the attitude of Ministers. There's a strong argument that commissioning / procurement of social care is the most important procurement issue in the UK public sector today. That's at several levels, from the growing billions that are being spent, to the wider social effects, potential issues and benefits.

Yet, where is the drive from the top to put some effort into this area? Where is the analysis of what works / doesn't work around the country from a procurement perspective? The promulgation of best practice? Development of innovative solutions, service providers and contracting mechanisms? Training of commissioners and social care procurement staff? The development of contract management standards and reporting?

Meanwhile, Francis Maude and some of the very best brains in public sector procurement are getting stuck in – harmonising the prices of toner cartridges, to keep Sir Philip Green happy, and making sure all Whitehall civil servants book their hotels through the same firm.

Perhaps it's time there was a discussion about priorities here?

***

I've always been a big fan of public procurement, having worked in line management, interim and consulting roles around the sector for many years. I know how difficult it is. But I suppose inevitably, I have written a lot about things going wrong, or made criticisms – constructive, I hope – of what was going on. The efforts to increase spend with smaller suppliers was a regular topic, and I exposed the dodgy data that continued to be presented. Then there was the expensive West Coast Rail franchise fiasco.

Report into West Coast Rail Franchise – Yes, It Was a Fiasco

Sam Laidlaw, a Department for Transport (DfT) non-executive director, published the interim report into the West Coast Rail franchise issues yesterday. I've just had a quick read through, and it is a real shocker. Arguably worse than I expected, for one key reason: this wasn't 'just' a genuine error in a spreadsheet, but rather the Department choosing to proceed with the competition, even though it knew it was flawed in one key respect.

DfT was aware that its model to calculate the Subordinated Loan Facility (SLF), which would give the government comfort that the bidder could withstand downturns, was not fit for purpose, having been originally designed for other purposes. But rather than sort this out, or disclose the issue to bidders, they decided to try and get away with it. There were then three problems:

1. This model for internal use wasn't disclosed to bidders. Instead, a 'ready reckoner' was provided to bidders to try and reassure them that they didn't need to see the 'real' model. That invited a challenge straight away, even if nothing else had gone wrong, because the bidders could reasonably claim they didn't have transparency around how their bid would be evaluated (lesson 1 in 'how to run a tender that will get challenged').

2. But then neither of these two models – the internal one or

the ready reckoner – was actually used once the bids came in, in direct contradiction of the published evaluation methodology! Instead, the Department appears to have invented some new way of calculating the required SLF – it's not yet clear to me exactly what that mechanism was – but it led to 'inconsistent treatment of First and Virgin'.

3. And, if I'm reading it correctly, if they had used the model that they said they would, officials would have misunderstood the data anyway because they thought the output was expressed in nominal terms when the model actually calculated it in real terms (regarding future inflation).

What a mess. Laidlaw's initial analysis of why this happened supports some of our early theories we published a few weeks back:

- He talks about the change in structure in DfT whereby no single Directorate had responsibility (my comment – 'Rather than a single Rail Directorate, responsibility seems to be spread across several areas').
- He mentions a loss of capability (as I said, 'just those four guys represented a huge loss of corporate memory, knowledge, wisdom and experience in the rail and franchising area, all disappearing within months of each other').
- And then there are the rushed nature of the programme, headcount reductions, and lack of consulting support in key areas – all arguably consequences of the cost reduction programme, as we suggested ('the reduction in consulting spend in government has had at least some negative consequences').

I didn't know, however, until this report that the programme had three senior responsible officers through the competition's relatively short life – a good indicator of likely disaster. One other point: it's clear some defensive drawbridges have already come down. From the report:

> 'parallel employment-related investigation has meant that witness interviews so far conducted have been subject to constraints.'
>
> 'the Inquiry team has not been given access to certain of the DfT's external lawyers because of concerns as to a possible waiver of legal professional privilege.'
>
> 'Ernst and Young has not yet been given access by the DfT to the full base case and risk-adjusted bidder models.'

So, the central questions in terms of blame allocation will be these:

- What was the decision-making process, and who signed off the decision to carry on with the competition despite the known issue with the internal model?
- Who accepted the obvious risk of challenge because of the lack of transparency in use of the various models?
- Who then decided to calculate the SLF figures in a different way entirely?
- Was there institutional bias against Virgin (that is hinted at in the interim report but not made explicit)?

Those first two are such fundamental issues, I would be amazed if approval didn't go up to Ministerial or at least Permanent Secretary level for sign-off. And I'd love to see the legal advice (assuming there was some) in terms of the challenge issue. But certainly, when I was a Procurement Director in government, I wouldn't have taken responsibility for those sorts of decisions on my own, knowing that if it went wrong, I'd be in the newspapers or worse!

***

And then there was the ongoing failure of the UK government to hit its own targets for spending with smaller suppliers.

Departments Declare Dodgy SME Data

At the risk of losing friends in Cabinet Office, we must sadly report that the recent claims that there has been a dramatic growth in government spend with small suppliers (SMEs) are, I'm afraid, unsafe. That doesn't mean they're incorrect – but it's clear that the data is not good enough to say with any scientific certainty (or even reasonable probability) that the claims are sound.

We reported last week on the Ministry of Defence, who with commendable honesty admitted that they couldn't explain the apparent growth in spend with SMEs and it might result from changes in the way the numbers are measured.

Now we've had our Freedom of Information response from the Ministry of Justice (MOJ), the other Department that apparently showed a huge increase in spend according to the Cabinet Office. One element that we thought suspect was the inclusion in the latest data of smaller law firms who provide legal aid services – we reckoned they weren't included in previous years' figures.

This was confirmed by MOJ in their reply to us. 'I can confirm that Legal Aid providers have been in our returns since the start of the 2011/12 financial year'.

So, there's one obvious reason for the significant apparent growth in the SME figure. Some of the law firms listed as SMEs are also not exactly what we'd normally think of as SMEs, even if they might technically fit the criteria – Tuckers, for instance, with around 200 fee-earners, are not exactly tiny!

But more serious doubts emerge from the list of the top 50 SMEs by spend provided to us by MOJ. They included names such as Service Support (Avon & Somerset) Ltd – the MOJ's largest 'SME' supplier last year – and Modern Courts (East Anglia) Ltd).

When we looked into these, it's clear that they are Private Finance Initiative 'special purpose vehicles', formed to run the PFI projects for building / rebuilding and management of courts around the country. These are multimillion-pound contracts, requiring serious financial strength, and as such, they are generally owned by a consortium of large firms – Laing and Mowlem being two lead examples in these cases.

I questioned MOJ on this and their response was 'Dun & Bradstreet have informed us they are SMEs'. Now, as an ex-D&B Procurement Director myself, I'd be interested to know how such organisations are being classified in this way! But I find it hard to believe this is correct even technically, and by no stretch of the imagination are they what Francis Maude or David Cameron are thinking about when they talk about their (genuine) desire to see more spend going to smaller firms.

We've also seen another Department who appear to be classifying all spend on Procurement Cards as 'SME spend' but we need to look into that a little more carefully before naming names.

But anyway, the clear message is this. The data isn't good enough at the moment to show clear trends, growth or otherwise, so claims on SMEs need to be taken with a veritable de-icing-the-M25 quantity of salt!

***

Why Isn't Government SME Spend Increasing?

Recent figures showed that spend with SMEs in central Government isn't increasing and, in some Departments, has declined. We shouldn't be surprised at this. Arguably, some of the initiatives started by this Government – and let's give them credit for taking some new and useful actions – haven't had time to come through yet in terms of the required outcome of greater spend with SMEs.

But my hunch is that the Whitehall numbers will continue to be disappointing through this parliament. That's why there has been subtle (or not so subtle) moving of the goalposts. It is now an 'aspiration' to increase SME spend 'over the course of the parliament', and that even now 'includes spend in the supply chain', which is a meaningless concept.

Just to highlight that – what if a large firm subcontracts to an SME, but 75% of the SME's revenue is spent with their own suppliers – who are large firms? How much of that counts as 'SME spend'? And if the SME subcontracts to another SME, do we count that spend twice? That would certainly improve the numbers.

But it demonstrates the illogicality of this approach. That's not to say that encouraging SME participation down the supply chain isn't a good thing – it is. But, to be blunt, basing your target on it is a sign of desperation.

Anyway, we've some up with 10 reasons why we believe central government will struggle to hit the target over the next three years or so.

1. There are many long-term legacy contracts in Government that even if an organisation wanted to get out of and substitute with lots of smaller SME friendly contracts, they can't. Or at least not without great problems or cost. For a large department, over 50% of

the spend is probably tied up in 3-year or longer contracts.

2. Then there's an even more onerous and inflexible form of 'legacy contract' – the PFI (Private Finance Initiative) contract. Here, it is pretty much impossible even to renegotiate the price for changing a light bulb, let alone anything significant that might help the SME numbers. With an outstanding PFI commitment of billions still (not all of it in central Government by any means of course) there's a huge chunk of future spend that isn't going to find itself anywhere near an SME.

3. Central Government is by its very nature big, even more so in the UK than many other countries of our size who have a stronger regional model. Where we take a national approach to a topic like benefits, for instance, you inherently end up with large, national benefits systems and therefore contracts to develop and support them. And some stuff central Government buys is just unavoidably huge – any SMEs want to build an aircraft carrier? Or an Olympic stadium? And this is not improving – in fact, with new investment appearing to focus on grandiose schemes such as high-speed rail, SMEs are not going to see this situation improving.

4. Most civil servants – and many politicians – are risk-averse by nature. 'No one ever got fired for buying IBM' is still a prevalent attitude. Who is going to take the risk, for example, to break up a large Department's IT contract with Capgemini, HP or Accenture and split it into 100 pieces with various SMEs? Would you feel like taking that risk? And ironically, Ministers taking an anti-civil service stance makes things worse not better. Do you think that being called 'enemies of enterprise' by the PM made public procurement staff think, 'I must take some risks on exciting but unproven new SMEs

at once?!' Or was the attitude more likely to be 'no one likes us, better keep my head down, follow the standard process, and look for the early retirement deal / job with the private sector'. I suspect we can guess which was more usual.

5. While it is a minor point compared to some here, we've argued before that the move to 'eliminate PQQs' for lower value contracts does not necessarily help SMEs. It has led in some cases to a much greater bidding burden, where the single document now combines the PQQ questions AND the full tender. The bidder has to complete both – knowing that their tender response won't even be read if they fail on the PQQ section! In some cases, SMEs who would have completed a simple PQQ are choosing not to bid given the workload and the risk / reward balance of the new approach.

6. We're seeing more centralisation of procurement and aggregation of volume which tends to favour larger suppliers unless those doing the centralisation are very careful. Contracts end up being too large for SMEs to win in many cases. While organisations such as the Government Procurement Service (*which became Crown Commercial Service*) are aware of this danger and are working to avoid squeezing out smaller firms, organising procurement on a national basis across central government still has a real risk of ending up with larger, national suppliers dominating.

7. Two years of spending cuts in certain sectors has squeezed out SMEs already. While the public may feel delighted that spend on contractors, consultants, advertising agencies and recruitment firms has declined, these were actually industry sectors where SMEs are probably stronger than the average. SMEs in these areas who relied on government work have had to reorientate themselves or have

disappeared, so some SME capacity has probably gone from those markets completely.

8. The same spending squeeze has reduced the resource available within government organisations. So, they have been looking for ways of reducing workload. In the procurement space, that is leading to greater use of collaborative deals or more use of prime contractor-type arrangements. As an example, more and more organisations are using a 'vendor managed' service for engaging temporary staff. Whereas, previously, there might have been 50 different suppliers, many of them SMEs, now everything has to go through Capita, Comensura or Matrix. While this may be a sensible business and commercial decision, the SME spend recorded by that organisation will show a decline.

9. Large firms who do a lot of public sector business are, in general, good at selling to Government. They have friends in high places, they invest in the sector, and they're good at influencing the direction of government policy. SMEs generally don't have the time or money to do this. Perhaps now money is tighter, that competitive advantage of large firms becomes more pronounced. And, as we've said before, there is a risk that encouraging buyers to engage more with the market pre-procurement will play to the strengths of the larger suppliers.

10. The work on the 'Innovation Launch Pad' in Cabinet Office was promising. But while it is too soon to judge overall success, it's fair to say we aren't seeing a large volume of spend going to dynamic, innovative smaller firms as yet.

So, there is little prospect of the numbers in terms of spend with

SMEs suddenly improving anytime soon. That's why the 'moving the goalposts' strategy is being followed, as we said yesterday. If the government is serious, the only points that are relatively easily addressed would be around splitting contracts into smaller chunks – for instance, regional frameworks rather than a national approach. But that would be administratively expensive and, critically, might jeopardise the savings claims that are also a key driver for the government.

One final point. The wider, devolved public sector (councils, police, hospitals, schools) spends far more than central government and in many ways is a more promising option for SMEs. Now, not everything is rosy in those sectors either; but if they can support SMEs, that would more than compensate for disappointment in central government.

***

But I also had a go at those who I felt criticised public procurement unfairly. The illogicality in the File on 4 radio show, for instance, or the general media praise for Circle Health, the first private firm to run an NHS hospital, who made all sorts of claims about how great they were before – three years later – pulling out of the contract early!

Circle Healthcare and Hinchingbrooke – Simple Procurement Question, No Answer

There was a flood of publicity earlier this month about how Hinchingbrooke Hospital had been 'turned around by Circle in six months', as the *Telegraph* put it. Hinchingbrooke is the first National Health Service hospital to be 'outsourced' to a private sector provider (Circle Healthcare). The CEO of Circle, Dr Ali Parsa, appeared on the BBC – as they reported:

> Circle chief executive Ali Parsa said the company had saved £1.6m by ordering the hospital's paper supplies differently, and they had introduced the same management style used at their private hospitals.

Well, of course this got my interest. Saving £1.6 million on paper supplies! Incredible! How did they do that? I wondered. So, I asked Circle (by email). I stressed that I'm not anti-private healthcare (true). But, as I said in my request:

> What I would like to know is how you made this saving? It seems an awful lot of money to be spending (saving) on paper! Is that a saving in a single year or £160k a year multiplied over a 10-year contract? Was it a dreadful deal previously? Just a little more explanation would be very useful because our readers I'm sure would be interested in how you are improving procurement in this manner.

Two emails were read (according to Outlook) but nobody replied. I tried phoning the media contact given on their website. Got an answering service, no response. Tried the Head Office number on their website, no answer at all. That all makes me wonder about the firm generally, but coming back to the savings, I now see that on their website, it says '£1.1m procurement savings banked. £1.6m *identified* this year' (my highlighting).

Now that is VERY different from saving that much specifically on paper. I spoke to a friend of mine who is Head of Procurement for a significantly bigger hospital than Hinchingbrooke.

'We don't spend that (£1.6m) in total in a year including on medical pulp,' he said. And that's total spend remember, not 'savings'.

So, what are we to conclude? Well, in the absence of any evidence to the contrary offered by the firm, I'm making a bold statement – Circle will *not* save £1.6m on paper this year. But let's be charitable and assume that Dr Parsa just got a bit confused in the heat of the moment, and £1.6m identified savings in total came out as £1.6m 'on paper'. Strange mistake to make, but maybe in the heat of a live interview?

Because if we don't assume it was an honest mistake, it might look like he was misleading us in order to generate a snappy headline or paint a stronger picture of public sector procurement incompetence.

Now, as regular readers know, we can be as hard as anyone on public procurement when criticism is deserved. But what is really beginning to annoy me is people using dodgy data or dodgy analysis either to simply knock public procurement or to paint some fantastical picture of 'savings potential'.

Sir Philip Green of course did the same thing in 2010 with his review of the 'terrible waste' in public procurement. But it took months for the truth to come out – that at least some of his price benchmarking, that painted a picture of public procurement failings, was not based on like-for-like comparisons.

So whenever we see this sort of report, we must ask – is the data accurate? Is the analysis robust? Does the writer have a vested interest in painting a particular picture?

The problem is, by the time that the error is exposed, the *Daily Mail* or BBC website reader has long since moved on, to be left with just a slightly stronger impression of public sector incompetence. And that's not right. So, let's declare war on dodgy procurement figures, analysis or news, wherever it comes from.

***

File on 4

A BBC Radio File on 4 programme the other day looked at whether the UK could do more to support UK-based / local suppliers to win more government contracts.

It started with a contract for wheelie bins awarded by Durham City Council – to a French firm. Apparently, there was a UK bidder who offered lower prices – saving £250,000 – but they couldn't meet the required delivery dates. Now, my parents are Durham Council taxpayers and I think they might have hung on a little longer for a new bin if they'd known it was that much cheaper. Anyway, that suggests the 'problem' was the council didn't place *enough* weighting on price in the tender evaluation. The UK supplier might have won if a higher weighting had been given.

Then we had the contract for steel for the Forth Road Bridge. Here, it got a bit difficult, as it seemed to be primarily a Prime contractor issue – a Prime who had then sourced steel from Poland, Spain, China. And the contracting authority wasn't in a position to dictate to the Prime where they should buy from. But then the 'problem' was described as the weighting of cost at 92.5% in the tender – if it had been given a lower weighting and other factors considered, then the UK bidder might have won. So, I ended up a little confused.

You see the problem? In the first case, *more* weighting on price would have helped the UK supplier. In the second, a *lower* weighting would have helped. So, while it was all interesting stuff, what exactly was the programme suggesting? Other than a bit of retrospective fiddling of evaluation processes, which I suspect many people would like, it's hard to see how we can square that particular circle to help UK bidders.

There was then some discussion of the way that some countries, like France, make it a requirement to split contracts into smaller lots when feasible – certainly not something that has been done in most of the UK, which, if anything, has gone in the opposite direction.

But the heart of the programme, which included ideas that are more applicable generally, came when we moved on to the work undertaken by public sector procurement in Wales. Their 'community benefit' strategy asks potential suppliers to respond to tender questions that are within EU regulations but support local communities and businesses.

For example – 'state how you will actively participate in economic regeneration activities' or 'provide a plan for how you will utilise unemployed people…'

You have to be careful how you ask such questions so they're not perceived as discriminatory, but the point was (well) made that there is a lot you can do without crossing the line and breaking the regulations.

Now this all sounds great and I've personally got a lot of time for what has been done in Wales. But of course, it does beg some questions. When the interviewer asked a guy from Costain (who won a roads contract that asked various community benefit questions) whether they'd upped the price because of all these 'extras', he got a not particularly convincing response. And price was weighted at only 20% in that particular tender – we didn't even hear whether Costain's was the cheapest bid.

So, do we have any evidence as to whether this policy is costing Wales more money than the traditional approach? If so, how much? Do we have evidence as to what it is doing on the benefit side – has unemployment decreased faster in Wales than in other comparable UK areas?

That's the sort of research and analysis that someone should be doing, as it looks like Wales has been an excellent test bed for this approach. If the Welsh experience is delivering real benefits, then let's do it everywhere. But we need some more evidence, we'd suggest.

***

Finally, two articles concerning ex-Prime Minister David Cameron. I pointed out how difficult his negotiations with the EU would be, particularly as he was making it harder by his own actions. I was right: he didn't get much in the way of concessions from the EU, which ultimately led to the UK Referendum and the travails that followed. And I wasn't very happy with him deciding that public procurement people were 'enemies of enterprise'. My response to that in the form of a letter to him (included here) cost me my non-executive role with a government organisation, too. So much for the independence of non-execs!

David Cameron – Why His EU Negotiation May Fail

Everyone thinks they're a good negotiator. Well, certainly every *man* I've ever met (women tend to be more realistic about their abilities, I've found). Yet, if you ask a few questions, their ideas on what makes them so skilled are usually formed around the vaguest of concepts such as 'I'm tough' or 'I drive a hard bargain' or 'I always start with a really low offer'.

Yet the academic theory behind negotiation is solid, and there are some clear best practices in the field. But most people who consider themselves expert have no idea of the theory that underpins good practice. In particular, I wonder whether politicians receive any negotiation training? Or is it supposed to be something that comes naturally to them, like kissing babies and looking concerned when local voters bend their ears about arguments with the local council?

We have asked this before – we were concerned about the tactics being used in negotiations around civil service pensions, for instance, where threats were made against the trade union side that were clearly never going to be followed, though. Not a good approach, as any negotiator, or indeed parent to a toddler will tell you.

Now we see another example of what certainly looks like poor negotiation practice from our esteemed Prime Minister no less. He is going to enter negotiations with the EU on the UK relationship, powers that might be returned, budgets, and so on. But he is now making public statements around how great the EU is for the UK, how much he really wants to stay part of it, and so on.

This seems to be subverting his own BATNA – 'best alternative to a negotiated agreement'. The BATNA, both real and apparent, largely dictates the strength of your negotiation position. Cameron's BATNA is what he (and the UK) will do if the EU simply says 'non' to our requests for power to be returned, lower contributions or whatever.

In other words, to get the best deal for the UK, the PM needs his European 'opponents' in the negotiation to generally believe that he has an alternative, which must include ultimately walking away altogether. So, every time he says how much he wants to stay, he weakens his own negotiation position.

Perhaps he's following the negotiation tactic that many of us may even have used, which goes along the lines of 'Look, I want to do this deal, but my boss won't let me unless you give us another 5% discount.'

In Cameron's case that would be: 'Look, I want to stay in the EU, but the British people will only do that if I get another £5 billion a year back from you.'

But the big flaw in that approach is that it positions the negotiator as powerless – the classic response in business negotiations is to say,

'OK, let me negotiate with your boss, then.' In a political situation, I suspect the opponent will simply call your bluff.

Cameron should be positioning that the UK is pretty relaxed about leaving the EU – that our BATNA looks pretty good, and acceptable to the mass of UK voters. And note that it is the *perceived* situation that is important – not any underlying, heart-of-heart beliefs. But you have to be convincing with your presentation of your position and your alternatives. At the moment, Cameron's public remarks are not preparing the ground as well as they might for a successful negotiation.

There is one further issue here of course. This assumes that the EU negotiators *want* the UK to stay. If they have different objectives, or are simply neutral, then Cameron is in a fundamentally weak position. So, it is in the EU's advantage to develop their own BATNA, which would be: 'we don't really care if you're in or out!'

And if that were genuinely the case, Cameron will have a real problem in extracting any significant concessions.

***

Enemies of Enterprise

Dear Prime Minister,

As an ex-senior civil servant in a procurement role, and ex-President of the leading procurement professional body, I felt I should defend my friends and colleagues from your attack this week during your spring conference speech. Calling public procurement staff 'enemies of enterprise' was unfair and inappropriate, particularly as you know they are not well placed to respond, given their roles as civil and public servants. Indeed, that aspect of picking on those who cannot defend themselves was particularly disappointing.

Here are the points I would suggest you consider before you address this issue again.

1. Do you really think procurement people in Government come into work thinking, 'Today I'll stop some enterprising young company from succeeding'? Of course they don't. Every procurement person I know in the public sector wants to do a good job for their organisation and their country; and they often stand as a bulwark against potential corruption or waste of public money. In addition, there has been excellent work done in many public organisations already, usually driven by procurement, to encourage SMEs; I could give you many examples if you are interested.

2. That procurement role – helping to drive value for money and working within the law – is critical because in the vast majority of cases, procurement people are working for internal 'customers': the managers who actually hold the budgets. In my experience, it is often procurement that encourages a wider supply base, output-based specifications and similar, while the budget holder is saying, 'Just place a contract with the same big firm who has done it before.' Yes, procurement will also try and ensure that laws are not broken, but you should see procurement as a potential ally in achieving your goals, not your enemy.

3. The main cause of what you perceive as 'bureaucracy' in the procurement process is the EU procurement regulations. Most procurement professionals would be very happy to see them abolished, simplified or downplayed. What are you as Prime Minister doing about this? There are no signs as yet of your Government challenging the EU on anything, let alone something as fundamental as public procurement regulations. Clearly, you feel

that picking a fight with public procurement staff is easier than doing the same with Brussels!

4. But even if we didn't have EU regulations, procurement people have – and should have – an overriding aim to spend public money wisely. Giving contracts to exciting, 'innovative' companies who don't have a track record and can't objectively show that they deserve to win those contracts leads very quickly to corruption, fraud and misuse of public funds. And you know as well as I do, the minute that some scandal comes to light (and it will), politicians will pin the blame very firmly on the poor procurement officer, who decided to 'take a risk' with an interesting-looking small company that turns out to be incompetent, corrupt, or owned by the Minister or Council Leader's mistress. Encouraging risk-taking in procurement will lead not just to legal challenges and huge fines for public bodies; it will lead to some interesting scandals on the front pages.

5. And finally, your proselytising for small suppliers does not sit well with the almost daily exhortations from your Ministers for police forces, councils, or central Government Departments to come together, collaborate, and use their 'buying power' to try and get better deals by awarding bigger contracts. This will almost inevitably mean larger suppliers will gain; they are better positioned than smaller, innovative or young firms as contracts get larger and scope of provision wider. You can't have it both ways.

We all know of course that public procurement can be improved; no one is denying that. And I am impressed by much of the work going on in Cabinet Office to achieve that; I also know Francis Maude is more engaged with public procurement than any Minister has ever been.

But this was an unworthy comment, made to score political points at the expense of a group of professionals who share the same aims as you – to see their organisations get the best possible value from suppliers to the public sector. I don't expect it to happen, but I believe you owe procurement professionals in the public sector an apology.

Yours faithfully,

Peter Smith MA FCPIS

***

Chapter 5

ADVICE AND
GOOD PRACTICE

Here is a selection of the advice that I've offered over the years, all of it gratefully received and implemented by the procurement profession … or maybe not! We'll start with the work of Nobel Prize-winner Daniel Kahneman and how behavioural psychology plays into negotiation theory and practice.

Thinking (about Procurement) Fast and Slow
with Daniel Kahneman

Procurement is a relatively non-academic and unscientific 'profession'.

It lacks the regulatory basis of accounting, or a body of knowledge that is clearly laid out, agreed and codified as the correct way of doing things. It lacks the direct measurement of sales and marketing; we may not consider these business functions are particularly scientific, but actually they provide their disciples with direct ways of measuring the benefits of what they so, through metrics such as market share, customer awareness or simply sales figures.

The tangible nature of those results means that classical scientific experimentation is at least possible in these areas. The Brand Manager can try controlled alternative approaches and actually measure which one works best.

Procurement has very little in the way of scientifically proven best practice, and not really very much even in terms of academic underpinning to what we do day-to-day. That is in part because many key procurement activities appear highly subjective and are linked to behavioural skills and issues, which are harder to analyse and study than fact-based actions. Such 'soft' activities include negotiation, relationship management, even, arguably, risk management.

However, a very interesting addition to the 'scientific' basis for what we do has come from an unlikely quarter. Daniel Kahneman is a psychologist by training but won the Nobel Prize in Economics in 2002. He won that for showing that one of the foundations on which classical economics was built is faulty. That is the assumption that people behave as rational beings when it comes to economic behaviour and decisions. He and his collaborators proved that this is far from the case, which punched holes in much economic thinking and many existing theories.

But his work has far wider ramifications than 'just' classical economic theory. His book, *Thinking, Fast and Slow,* brings together his life's work in a highly readable (but not dumbed down) manner, and aims to explain, basically, how we think. It is brilliant, and I cannot recommend it highly enough.

At the heart of it is Kahneman's concept of System 1 and System 2 thinking. System 1 is the easy, automatic, intuitive, rapid thinking that gets us through most of life. Driving to work without thinking about the route. Answering most emails. Skim-reading documents. Recognising our families and close friends.

System 2 is the 'hard', out of our comfort zone, thinking. Answering difficult maths questions, responding to a tricky interview question, thinking hard about future procurement strategies perhaps.

So, one of his hypotheses, pretty well proven, is that we will do pretty much anything we can to avoid System 2 thinking, because it is difficult, uses more energy, and stops us multitasking. This goes right back to evolutionary thinking – we needed to do many things automatically to survive, and we couldn't be doing anything directly productively whilst engaged in System 2 thought. If we can think in an intuitive, rapid manner, without really engaging our full brainpower, we will.

We therefore rely on System 1 most of the time. And that means we are vulnerable to making all sorts of errors. We are easily manipulated, we are suggestible, we jump to conclusions, fail to calculate risk or probability properly, are influenced by irrelevant factors ... That list might begin to explain why classical economic theorists got very nervous about Kahneman's work. They had worked on their assumptions of the 'rational individual', which he said doesn't exist. It might also start to suggest why it also has major implications for us in procurement, and indeed anyone in business.

Let's finish for now with some of Kahneman's areas of study and concepts.

Priming – how we are influenced by everything around us, consciously and subconsciously, and the impact this has on our thinking and ability to carry out rational decision-making. It has implications for many procurement activities, from negotiation to tender evaluation and supplier selection.

Anchoring – a variant of Priming, this is the way in which our thinking is guided and even constrained by the information that is put in front of us. This has major implications for negotiation, in particular, but also for supplier management and other situations.

Jumping to conclusions – how our brains construct simple narratives whenever possible, resulting in poor ability to analyse and forecast properly. It has implications for negotiation, how we manage contracts and suppliers, and how we handle risk.

Attitude to risk – the work that won Kahneman his Nobel Prize was largely in this area. He showed how most people have 'illogical' attitudes to risk, and how this can lead to poor economic, personal or business decisions. This has implications not only for supply chain risk management (obviously), but also for many of our procurement strategies and activities.

***

Priming

Our last article introduced Daniel Kahneman's brilliant *Thinking, Fast and Slow* book. It explains how humans really think and behave, which turned out to be quite differently to how that was treated in classical economic theory.

One of the key areas of research and insight for Kahneman was that of 'priming', and priming effects. We'll highlight just some of the implications for procurement professionals.

If I show you the word EAT, then ask you to fill in the missing letter here; S O _ P, you are more likely to say 'SOUP' than 'SOAP'. If I had said 'WASH' initially, the opposite is true. That is priming – the idea of EAT primes the idea of SOUP. And it is an incredibly and almost unbelievably powerful effect.

It is not limited to words – it applies to actions and emotions, too. Experiments have shown that people primed with images of money act more selfishly after that priming; in the US, a vote on increasing funding for schools got more support where the polling station was in a school building.

Priming even works where we're not consciously aware that we have seen or heard something. Anyone in the UK who has seen Derren Brown's amazing 'tricks' will have seen this at work – he can apparently read the minds of his audience 'victims', but much is achieved by clever priming through words or images – often the subject doesn't even realise they have experienced this before coming onstage!

This is all caused by our System 1 thinking, looking to construct shortcuts and easy ways of operating. So, if I ask you to name an animal, and you've just seen a cat run across the road, System 1 says 'cat'. If there were pictures of cats in the reception area before you meet me, and even if you're not consciously aware you saw them, again you are likely to say 'cat'.

I would urge everyone to read Kahneman's book, but we can start to see how this concept might be both useful to us in procurement and might have some risks as well. We are very susceptible to being pushed into thinking or feeling in a certain manner – so how might a supplier take advantage of that? Well, they could look to prime certain feelings if the buyer is visiting their premises. Perhaps a noticeboard in reception with stories of collaboration, generosity, and kindness to prime those feelings in the buyer?

If the supplier is looking for a price increase, getting words like 'increase' and 'higher' in front of the buyer before the discussion might help – I know some of this seems far-fetched, but read the book and you will believe. And it is not totally new thinking – in a sense, we've talked about 'conditioning' in the context of negotiation for many years. Kahneman has brought more rigour and academic backing to some of that very thinking.

Priming can also help new firms or potential suppliers. Simply getting a name in front of people makes them feel more positive and comfortable about it, compared to something they haven't seen before. This is called the 'mere exposure' effect – as mere exposure to something makes us feel more positive about it.

In one experiment, invented words were printed – with no

explanation – in a student magazine. When subjects were shown these words, along with other made up words that had not been featured in the magazine, they had significantly more positive view of the words they had seen before – even though they were meaningless. We are simply more comfortable with repetition: 'words you have seen before are easier to see again', as Kahneman puts it.

So, in procurement, we need to be careful when we are looking for new suppliers or assessing bids and tenders. We are easily primed: we almost certainly have a built-in favouritism to incumbent suppliers, for instance, simply because we know them, their names and people. The easy System 1 decision is to go with what we know and find familiar. And if we don't have an incumbent, the firm whose name we have seen, even without any accompanying description of their capabilities, stands a better chance than one we haven't come across before.

There's also an interesting consequence for individuals. Let's say you're applying for a job. If you can somehow 'prime' the interviewer, this will help your chances. Simply phoning up, perhaps to confirm the time or some detail of the interview (you don't have to say anything particularly insightful), will make them feel better inclined towards you. And we could use this in terms of our stakeholder engagement strategy internally – contacting people before you turn up for an important meeting or discussion, particularly if they don't know you already, puts them in a better frame of mind for dealing with you positively.

There are many more examples of priming I'm sure that we could come up with in a procurement context. It's a fascinating topic, but only one of many described in *Thinking, Fast and Slow*.

***

158

Sometimes, I feel very confident giving advice, and sometimes I feel that the procurement world makes assumptions that don't really stack up to analysis or real-life experience. Here are a couple of examples.

Don't Overestimate Economies of Scale

Why do we assume that bigger is better in procurement terms? That, if I aggregate my spend, if I have more volume to offer the market, then I will get a better deal? Why should this be so? It can only be because the supplier benefits from the economies of scale that the greater volume offers them, and they can pass some of that benefit back to me in the form of better value.

There is no natural law that says a supplier must offer lower prices to a bigger buyer. If their unit cost for every item sold was independent of volume, there would be no reason for them to offer better pricing for more volume. They must benefit.

This basic belief in economy of scale underpins so much of what goes on in procurement; collaborative initiatives in the public sector, centralisation in large corporates, attempts to standardise specifications. Yet procurement and organisations generally often don't think very hard about how the concept applies to different markets or suppliers.

'Economies of scale' refers to reductions in unit cost as an organisation's scale of output increases. And of course, a larger volume on offer will in most cases have some economy of scale benefit. For a start, the sales cost per unit usually decreases; although it may not if a large contract has a very expensive bidding process attached (as is often the case in the public sector!)

That benefit to the supplier can come from a number of sources. It may, for instance, be a manufacturing economy or procurement economies in terms of buying raw materials; producing thousands of identical cars, or laptops, has obvious scale efficiencies. So, the ultimate customer can exploit that to get better pricing. But even those economies may depend on how similar the product is; hence why a generic discount from an auto manufacturer to a large fleet buyer, applicable to anything they buy, will fall well short of what they will offer for a definitive order covering 1,000 identical vehicles.

It may be economies in the sales process; the 'manufacturing' cost of software licences is basically zero, but you can get a great deal for volume purchases because you save the supplier a lot in terms of their marketing and sales effort, which is a major part of their cost base. It could be economies in financial terms: a large firm can get access to funds at a favourable rate to finance investment, which enables them again to pass on some of that benefit to the purchaser.

But procurement often makes the mistake of thinking that economies of scale apply everywhere, and in the same sort of manner. If I can get a 50% discount for volume from the software firm, why can't I get that from the facilities management provider if I offer them a big enough deal?

The simple answer is that the direct costs of the FM provider, particularly people, are relatively fixed per unit of output. The cleaning service provider might buy cleaning fluid slightly better as their volume goes up; but 60% of their price to you is direct labour, probably people working at minimum wage. Their scope to make economies of scale is limited as, therefore, is their ability to offer you a better deal in return for volume.

And there are some spend categories or products where we can even see diseconomies of scale; or other factors that mean the buyer with less volume on offer can do a better deal than the big buyer. Professional services spend is an interesting case. For many consultancy providers, for instance, economies of scale are principally around the utilisation at a consultant by consultant level.

You will therefore get a much better rate engaging a single consultant full-time for a given number of days – say, 200 – than for 20 consultants for 10 days each over the same period. That is one of the reasons why basic day-rate framework rates for consulting firms rarely show much reduction from rate card. But a major assignment that utilises staff on a close to full-time basis has more scope for negotiation.

Ask a large hotel to quote a room rate for 100 rooms; it won't be as good as the deal you MAY be able to negotiate on the day (if they have surplus capacity). It may not even be as good as the rate they will quote you for 10 rooms. Logically, if you buy a supplier's entire output, they must charge you an *average price* that enables them to make an adequate return; hence the rate for 100 rooms may not be as good as you expect. That is not the case if you are buying a small quantity of marginal volume (as in the case of the hotel).

I remember hearing that a buying consortium of airlines found exactly this issue when they tried to do 'group deals' with hotels around major airports. Their combined volume was too much; it eliminated some hotels from the market altogether; it would have stopped others from doing lucrative conference business (as 50% of their rooms would have been taken by the consortium). If they bid at all, they offered 'average' pricing. Individual airlines, looking for perhaps a few hundred room nights a year, rather than thousands, could get a better deal.

A buyer with smaller volumes can also often move more quickly to take advantages of market or supplier movement; and can use smaller providers who may just not be an option for the big buyer.

I once bought a raw material where I was an attractive but not huge buyer in market terms. We bought very tactically and aggressively using short-term contracts of 1-3 months (we would have used reverse auctions if the technology had been invented!)

The really big buyers in this market could not afford to take the risk of buying in this manner; and as they were buying perhaps 50% of the entire output of a production facility, they ended up paying very much a standard market price; we had independent evidence that we bought 10-20% better than our larger competitors.

Now, we're being provoking here. There are other benefits of aggregating and collaborating in procurement, including a time and cost saving on the procurement side, and using procurement expertise in the best possible way. But assuming that economies of scale apply uniformly, or that the bigger buyer will always do better than the smaller, is lazy thinking. We have to look at each category and product on its own merits.

***

Never Tell the Supplier Your Budget – Really??

This is one of those bits of good practice guidance that we are often given in negotiation training sessions or receive from the procurement mountain top like the wisdom of the ancients, or even see in textbooks.

'Never tell the supplier your budget.'

Now, clearly there are times when this is good advice, but we'd argue there are probably almost as many where it isn't. Let's start with the times it *is* sensible. If you're buying a defined quantity of items where you have little idea what a fair cost might be, and where there isn't much competition, then exposing the budget is likely to mean you've set a floor for the price. So, a bespoke piece of equipment, or maybe some software development where you're locked into a supplier might fall into this category.

'How much will this enhancement cost? My budget is £50k.'

'That will be £49,500.'

It is also pointless (or worse) if you have a lot of clarity on the quantity and quality of what it is you want, and a competitive market. So, if you can clearly define, 'I want three hundred laptops to that specification,' or even (in a less tangible spend category), I want a report from the lawyers that covers x, y and z, then you can let competition drive a best value response.

BUT ... there are times when disclosing your budget makes a lot of sense. Going back to first principles, there are two ways of approaching a competition. You can define what it is you want, and let the suppliers compete on price (and maybe other value-related factors of course). In effect, you have fixed the specification – quality and quantity – and the selection variable is value / price.

Or, you can fix the *price* (and other value factors if appropriate) and let the competition be based on the quality / quantity of what is offered against that.

So, whilst we gave the legal services example above, there are many professional services cases where fixing the price makes a lot of sense. If you want a report that assesses strengths and weaknesses in your procurement function and provides a procurement transformation plan, then your specification may get responses from suppliers suggesting anything from a £10,000 project to a £1 million assignment.

If you know your budget is at most £30k, then you've wasted suppliers' time and ruled out what might have been strong potential providers. So, when you invite proposals, why not say, 'We expect your proposals to be in the £25-30k price range.' Then judge the bids on factors such as the quality of the proposals, the insight they show, and the depth of the firm's experience.

The same can work for tangible items. If the marketing department has a budget of £100,000 to buy promotional items to support a new product launch, then the simplest tender question is just: 'How many can you give me for £100k?'

Or you can construct the request in a manner that doesn't eliminate price completely from the evaluation process. 'We want to refurbish our office. We have 200 workstations, three meeting rooms … etc. Please note that whilst our maximum budget is £1 million, our tender evaluation will consider price as one of the key factors.'

The big advantage of exposing the budget is that it saves the market, and potentially you as the buyer, wasting time and effort on unrealistically high (or indeed low) bids. It enables you to obtain competition based on the quality and quantity of what is proposed rather than the price. And it is applicable in many situations.

So, '*never tell the supplier your budget*' should become 'think carefully about whether telling your suppliers the budget might lead to a stronger competition and better ultimate value'.

***

Outsourcing has been one of the hot business topics of the last 20 years or so, so I gave some advice on that, too. Then there is some good advice from the BBC on the same topic.

Making the Business Case for Outsourcing

We have considered previously the role that procurement can play in outsourcing transactions and why it is sometimes difficult for the function to establish that role. One early contribution procurement can make is in the development or analysis of the *business case* for outsourcing.

A typical case might be an organisation that perhaps perceives it is not making enough use of outsourcing, so the Board asks that a range of opportunities be considered, with some sort of review and proposal to come back to the Board for approval.

The second case occurs when procurement is involved directly in a specific outsourcing decision and has a chance to contribute to the development of the business case or the go / don't go decision. In either case, we would suggest there are a number of factors that should influence the decision in whichever direction.

The first factors are internally focused and relate to the current situation in the organisation.

What is the state of readiness of the function / process area to be outsourced?

This leads us straight into one of the most common outsourcing beliefs. It goes like this. 'Don't outsource a mess. You'll get an outsourced mess.' The argument goes that the organisation should work internally to bring the area at least up to a reasonable level before outsourcing, to improve the chances of successful transition. The other justification is the cost argument. You will pay a lot of money for the outsourcer to sort out your problems if you transfer a fundamentally inefficient operation.

Whilst the view is understandable, it can be challenged on two counts. We would argue that, sometimes, a really good outsourced service provider can turn 'a mess' into something very satisfactory or even better. The other dilemma is that sometimes an organisation really doesn't have the capability to improve the area in question. And if the only other ways to improve matters are expensive consultancy, or a long and expensive internal development programme, then yes, sometimes it can be better to outsource a mess. But these are matters that must be considered as part of the overall *outsource / don't outsource* decision. And in general terms, the outsourcing transaction for a process or area that is tolerably effective is likely to be easier.

How strategically important is the potential process/function/ area to the organisation?

The general view is that outsourcing is best when the area in question is not part of the core strategic proposition of the organisation. That is true in most cases. Look at it from the perspective of the organisation's own customers. If some key element of your purchase is actually the work of a third party, then why not go direct to the third party?

However, again, we can challenge this to some extent. Some organisations have changed the parameters of the debate by outsourcing virtually everything. In a sense, they are saying, 'Our core skill is in managing a complex network of outsourced service (or product) suppliers and pulling that together into an overall business proposition.' So, the key question is probably something more connected with competitive substitution – does outsourcing weaken the firm's market position or make it more likely that someone (and that could even be the outsourced provider) could negatively impact the organisation's strategic position?

Does the organisation have the capability to manage the service provider?

Surprisingly, this is often a major issue. It can be managed – through investment in additional resource if necessary – but we include it here if nothing else to point out that it needs consideration. Retaining an intelligent client function is critical, which might mean not transferring all employees in the area under consideration to the service provider. And if the outsource is so esoteric, specialist or difficult that managing the ongoing contract is a real concern, then the whole strategy needs to be questioned.

Then we have the cost / benefit financial factors to consider.

What are the likely cost savings from the outsource?

This is conceptually easy to understand, although obtaining the appropriate information to support a business case can be challenging. Clearly, service providers may offer savings through economies of scale, greater expertise, or innovation. Work will need to be done prior to the business case development, as this will inevitably form an important part of the analysis.

What other 'softer' benefits might arise from the outsource?

This might be (for instance) better customer service via a service provider with higher performance levels than have been achieved internally; greater innovation leading to top-line business gains; or the (somewhat mythical in our view) 'focusing on our core business'. On that last note, whilst there is no doubt that some organisations are overcomplicated and would benefit from some simplification – which might mean outsourcing certain parts of the business – our experience is that these 'core business' benefits are very hard to quantify before or even after the transaction.

What will the process of outsourcing cost?

One potential outsource some years back had a business case that was excellent in many ways. The supply market was competitive and capable, the business area clearly wasn't core, the staff would have been better off in the outsourced firm, and there were savings to be had. However, the sheer cost of the outsourcing process, both the transaction costs and compensating staff payments (for pension rights etc.) meant that the payback was not attractive. (Perhaps half a million upfront costs; 50k a year savings.)

Whilst outsourcing can be executed in the private sector at least in a quick and dirty manner, it's not advisable. So, the costs should not be underestimated in the business case, both those directly related to the project and any staff issues, or compensating recruitment that might have to take place (see comments above on the intelligent client).

And finally, we need to look at the market.

How attractive and established is the market for the type of outsourcing we require?

Clearly, a business case is likely to be more attractive when there is a mature, competitive market available for the services that are going to be transferred. That gives the outsourcer a choice of provider, making it more likely that a good 'fit' can be found; it suggests that there will be strong competitive pressure amongst providers which should drive value for money and performance; it provides some resilience for the future supply situation; and probably means that the market and providers are experienced in delivering the service successfully.

Being the first organisation in the world to outsource 'Service X' to a brand-new provider might just bring amazing competitive advantage. But we would suggest it is a brave CPO who recommends doing so, given the obvious issues.

***

'Second Wave' Outsourcing – Good Advice from the BBC

At the ProcureCon Indirect conference, Jim Hemmington, Procurement Director at the BBC, spoke about the organisation's experience through what is now a considerable history of outsourcing.

Hemmington personally and the BBC corporately now go back 10 years or more in terms of outsourcing some pretty strategic and important activities, ranging from transactional finance and HR, to specialist areas such as licence fee collection and transmission services.

What's interesting is how that considerable experience is now informing their latest strategies for what are second or even third time around outsourcing contracts and competitions. Hemmington passed on some valuable lessons learnt – here are just a few that seemed to have particular relevance to a wider audience.

1. Be very clear about the sort of relationship you need with your service provider. Not all outsourcing contracts require 'collaborative' supplier relationships – sometimes you just want a simple service, delivered well. But where the service is complex, critical or changing, you need to work hard to ensure you get real collaboration and the right relationship. That includes having focused contract and supplier management, with the right people, working in a consistent manner. 'The right people' also means understanding that some people are good at building relationships, some at managing tightly to a contract. Use their skills in the appropriate manner.

2. Negotiate agile contracts and look carefully at risk transfer. Hemmington explained that initially, in the first wave of outsourcing, the BBC very much looked to transfer risk to the supplier. But when risks became more manageable through the contract period, that approach meant the supplier obtained all the benefits of that reduced risk profile. So now the BBC looks more critically at which risks to retain itself and looks for contracts that have more flexibility to respond and vary as key influencing factors change through the contract period.

3. Cost transparency is key if there are likely to be changes through the contract period. Having that understanding of the supplier's cost structures helps the BBC to ensure fair outcomes (for both parties) when there are (for example) changes in demand or technology through the contract period. This again requires good contract management – even if you have strong initial competition, this is not enough to ensure value for money throughout the contract period.

There is food for thought there, as there was throughout the session. Hemmington emphasised that there is no single right approach to outsourcing, but these and other key principles, gained over some years of often tough experience, now seem to have put the BBC in a situation where they're managing their portfolio of outsourcing contracts pretty successfully.

***

But the advice was not always as serious as the last couple of examples. It is always good to find a piece of research that is possibly useful but also is a little more 'fun' than a debate about outsourcing!

Flirting for Procurement Professionals

So, after a huge research project, psychologists have discovered that women who 'flirt' as part of their negotiation strategy get better results than those who don't. Well, who would have thought it?!

Note that this wasn't something dreamt up by *Cosmopolitan* or the *Daily Mail* – this was serious academic research carried out by the University of California Berkeley and the London School of Economics. The title is 'Feminine Charm: An Experimental

Analysis of Its Costs and Benefits in Negotiations' and it has been published in the *Personality and Social Psychology Bulletin*. Here's a flavour of the abstract, showing the academic nature of the work.

> The authors examined feminine charm, an impression management technique available to women that combines friendliness with flirtation. They asked whether feminine charm resolves the impression management dilemma facing women who simultaneously pursue task (i.e. economic) and social goals in negotiations.

More interesting perhaps was the distinction drawn between flirting and being friendly. Merely being friendly, without any of what the researchers defined as flirting techniques, didn't work. The researchers talk about 'friendliness' signalling a concern for others, whereas being flirtatious is 'signalling a concern for self'.

The hypothesis is that friendliness increases likeability but also might indicate a weaker negotiating stance, if you are seen as less competitive and self-interested. Flirtation signals more concern for self, which could decrease likeability but might increase perceived negotiating strength. But this only works, according to the research, when the 'victim' is male, and the deals were worse if the flirting was perceived as merely being friendly. Here's how the researchers told female participants to turn on the charm.

> In the feminine charm condition, females were advised to be animated in their body movements, make frequent eye contact with their partner, smile, and laugh. They were further advised to be playful and to compliment their partner in as sincere a fashion as possible.

So, to negotiate successfully, women should use 'feminine charm', both friendly behaviour and flirtation – you're trying to be viewed as likeable but also motivated by self-interest. But joking aside, a couple of things worry me conceptually here. Firstly, I'm not totally clear how flirtatious behaviour indicates 'self-interest'. It almost seems like the opposite – doesn't it indicate an interest in the other party? Maybe that is why people respond positively in the negotiation? In an experiment carried out by *The Sun* newspaper, it seemed to be about a pretty girl taking an interest in the men with whom she was (pretty successfully) negotiating?

And clearly there were other ways to demonstrate self-interest in a negotiating situation, if that is the goal. Showing you have a strong BATNA (best alternative to a negotiated agreement), that you've researched the market or issue over which you're negotiating, expressing yourself confidently ... they would all seem to be good ways to show self-interest without fluttering your eyelashes. Having said that, I have found in real business situations that women who get the flirtatiousness just right can be very effective negotiators. But there's another danger there – overdo it, and it can be counterproductive!

Another point to note is that the experimental situation used in this study was buying a car, a one-off situation and not a typical business negotiation. Having said that, this is an interesting piece of research and one I'm sure will get many people talking. And Forbes magazine extrapolates further into workplace behaviour generally:

> Women who use feminine charm effectively with co-workers, bosses, and employees will convey the message that they are friendly but not overly accommodating.

***

I followed that up with a dramatic revelation, never before proposed in a professional procurement context ...

Flirting for Men

'Alan! Nice to see you! Must be – what two years? Maybe three? When we did that Glasgow deal together? You're looking good – have you been working out recently? No? Really, you've lost some weight, then. I like your shirt, by the way. Very smart. And, you lucky bu***r, you've still got your full head of hair. Wish I could say the same! And how's the wife? Yes? Good, and the kids are well, Jessica must be at university now? And how's the golf, still playing off single figures? You must come out with us sometime, we have a golf day at Sunningdale every year, really good, you're much better than me, of course, but it's a good laugh, few beers afterwards ...'

We recently described research that showed women who flirt as part of their negotiation strategy get a better deal than those who don't. Pure 'friendliness' is not enough either. So, does this put women at an advantage in negotiation? Well, not necessarily. But I have always, throughout my years in procurement, been surprised that there weren't more women in senior sales roles, because such a high proportion of the ones I have met were very good.

They possessed qualities such as empathy, persuasiveness, listening skills – and maybe at times there was an element of flirting, although I would stress that can't make up for someone who is incompetent or unreliable. (Some years back, I asked a sales director to remove a startlingly attractive, young saleswoman from our account, because she was, frankly, useless.)

But here's a dirty little secret. *Men flirt, too.* And not just when they're faced with a woman in a negotiating situation – but we flirt with other men. We don't call it flirting of course. We call it 'bonding' or 'building a relationship'. Or 'company golf days'. And it's not (or at least usually not) homoerotic in nature. But many of the best negotiators work to build a rapport and a warmth that, as the research suggested, needs to go a little beyond the mere 'friendliness'.

So, as per my little monologue above, we pay compliments. We make the flattering comparisons, ask solicitous questions about the family. There's the 'gift-giving', so key in many cultures, even if it is just a round of golf or even a pint of beer.

But just as the flirting research suggests, it can't descend into appearing weak. That's why there will often, alongside the flattery and jokiness, be an undercurrent of competition when two men are talking like this in a business situation.

'I'm jealous, Peter – you're still going to the gym twice a week? I wish I could, I've had terrible knee problems since I won the Ironman Triathlon last year, I'm afraid… might have to pull out of my charity stilt walk to the North Pole next month at this rate, but Luke, my six-year-old, can stand in for me. Did I tell you he's had trials for Barcelona …?'

So, we get the positioning for power and dominance, along with the establishing of rapport and warmth – quite a powerful combination for a negotiator.

But there is an alternative. Certain people I've met in my time – Sir Peter Gershon comes to mind, when he ran the UK Government Office of Government Commerce – made no effort to establish a relationship in most negotiation-type situations, yet could be highly effective. Flirting, it is probably fair to say, did not in my experience come naturally to Sir Peter. Yet he has had a stellar career and will go down in history as (I'm told) one of the few people whom 'Gordon Brown was scared of'. (Or at the very least, one of the few who wasn't scared of Brown.)

So, there's always another way of being successful in negotiation, business or life. But you knew that already, of course – I mean, I've always been amazed at how perceptive you are, you keep up with all the latest business thinking. You read a lot, don't you? I don't know how you find the time, I wish I could...

***

Back to the more serious stuff, and a selection of articles advising on procurement issues including category management, contingent fees and even tweeting! (Written in the early days of my Twitter life.) Let's start with some recruitment advice.

'People Are Our Biggest Asset'

'People, who need people, are the luckiest people in the world...' (*Funny Girl*, 1964, Styne and Merrill). If you think about it, aren't they the most stupid lyrics ever? What on earth does it mean? Why does needing something make you lucky? But enough, already ...

How often have you heard a senior manager, perhaps a procurement director, say that 'people are our biggest asset'? Or words to that effect. Yet ask a few questions and see if the reality lives up to the rhetoric. How much does the organisation invest in training? And I don't mean random 'I fancy doing this course on negotiation tactics learnt from the ancient Incas' training. I mean training based on a structured assessment of individual capability, followed by gap analysis linked to the procurement function's strategy and priorities.

And how seriously, really, does the organisation take recruitment? Is the agency appointed on the basis of the lowest cost offered? Do they understand procurement?

Mars, where I started my career, is the best organisation I've ever worked for, or with, and one of their '5 principles of Mars' is Mutuality – which means that everyone who comes into contact with the firm should benefit in some way. That led to Mars – certainly in my day – being an excellent firm in terms of recruitment practices.

Even those who didn't get a job walked away feeling positive, or at least that was the very direct objective. Why? Because that individual might spend 50p a day for the rest of their lives on Mars products – or not, if they felt they were badly treated. And that could add up to thousands of pounds, dollars or euros over a lifetime. Or they might turn out to be the next confectionery buyer for Walmart or Tesco.

So, I would argue that most organisations have a vested interest in treating people well in the recruitment process, and procurement people in particular should be handled with care. Yet I've heard two recent instances where this hasn't happened.

One is a 'solutions provider' – I won't be specific but think software, consulting, outsourcing etc. They work in the procurement space, and also regularly recruit procurement people. So, when an experienced professional tells me that this firm hasn't even replied to several applications, I wonder whether the recruiter considers the likelihood that this person will feel well intentioned if they ever find themselves possibly buying from the firm?

Perhaps even worse was a huge firm that sells to both corporates (usually through the procurement function) and individuals. Their recruitment process showed a combination of arrogance (not informing people whose CVs didn't make the cut) with incompetence (an online recruitment platform that was virtually incomprehensible). A friend of mine – who would, I guarantee, have been a perfect fit – was left vowing to a) never apply for a job there again; b) make life difficult for them in the corporate world given half a chance; and c) never buy their products again as a consumer.

That firm has suffered a huge fall from grace since then, losing their global market leading position. Incompetence and arrogance – a dangerous combination, I suspect.

So do just check how your recruitment process works and how applicant-friendly it is. For instance, if someone has bothered to apply, I do believe they deserve a reply, and preferably a brief explanation of why you rejected them. If you're a CPO, or a senior exec in a solutions provider, perhaps even put in a dummy application, and see how it looks from the outside …

And remember – annoying any business person is not a good idea; and annoying procurement people is even worse.

***

Contingent Fees Consulting – Take Care!

We wrote recently about the sad death at Glastonbury of Christopher Shale, who ran Oxford Resources, a cost-reduction consultancy. Like many such firms, they work largely on a contingent fee basis – they will take a share of the savings they find for their clients. Now that has some clear advantages: done properly, it is a guaranteed win for the clients. You only pay for the consultants if you make savings, there is (apparently) no risk, and you save a multiple of the fees you pay.

We said previously that Oxford were (are) a reputable firm. But there are some real sharks in that market, who will manipulate the contingent mechanism to their own advantage. And there are also some negatives about the process that buyers don't always consider. So, what could possibly go wrong with this approach?

Well, the consultant could find an alternative supplier at an apparently lower-price but with quality or service that does not live up to the previous supplier. That may not be apparent immediately – perhaps not until after the contingent fee has been invoiced and paid.

The consultant might even (and I have seen this happen) find a new supplier who will quote a very low price for long enough to enable the consultant to claim and extract their share of the 'savings' – but then the supplier withdraws or stops supplying. Collusion between consultant and supplier? I couldn't possibly comment!

Accurate baselining is obviously key to determining the starting point for any savings. Leaving that to the consultant is another risk if they are of the unscrupulous breed. Digging around to find the highest possible price paid for an item across an entire organisation, then using that as the baseline, is something else I've seen.

Then there are the issues that are not the consultant's fault but can make the share of savings route very costly. A new supplier or contract may be genuinely lower price, but procurement may have problems driving compliance across the organisation (particularly if there is a change in quality or specification). The share of savings calculation may assume 100% compliance with the new contract; but the actual performance may be very different.

Or the need for the product or service may change over time, making the 'saving' less relevant – which can be a problem if the share of savings payment has been based on a three-year period.

Finally, the amount payable to the consultants may just exceed all expectations. Now that may sound great – look at all the money we've saved – but if the contract is based on paying the consultant before the savings are genuinely realised, the size of the payment may cause some embarrassment internally.

I heard of one case where an energy consultant (and I should say this is an area that actually suits contingent fee mechanisms pretty well) found a long-running billing error for their financial services client. That saved the firm huge amounts, but the client baulked at paying an invoice for several hundred thousand pounds. After all, they argued, the consultants 'had only done a couple of weeks' work'. I believe the case ended up in court – and the consultant got their money, quite rightly.

There is a time and a place for this type of approach – but do take care.

***

Why You Should Tweet

I've been tweeting for a few months now, and I'm a Twitter fan, although not an obsessive. So here is my view as a user and procurement professional on good reasons why you should consider doing the same.

Fast access to information including of business relevance
Twitter reported Osama bin Laden's killing before conventional media. Learn about global events, or, more directly usefully, what key suppliers are up to before anyone else.

Useful info for day-to-day life
When we had the snow earlier this year, we were due to go into London and the train websites were suggesting that trains into London were only being delayed slightly. I searched for 'southwest trains' on Twitter and found about a dozen tweets from people saying, 'I've been stuck on this train outside Clapham for an hour ...' We decided not to bother.

Point you towards latest thinking
If you follow the right people, you'll get told about lots of new

reports, thinking, articles and other intellectual property. Check out the links and decide whether it's worth reading. Twitter gives you good signposting.

Be part of the community

This is more nebulous but there is a community – or rather a huge number of communities – on Twitter. They gossip, swap information, exchange views. It would be good to build a stronger procurement community. You can also indulge your guilty pleasures – want to swap views with like-minded fanatics about American Idol? Aston Villa Football Club? The Wine Society? John Prescott? You can. Tell people about Reading Festival highlights as they happen?

And while the good outweighs the bad, there's one particular negative with Twitter as well. It can take over your life. I follow 130 people, probably too many, and I could spend all day reading the latest news and thoughts about business, sport, music and arts, food, friends, sponsors etc. It's easy to get obsessed, so while I do recommend it, you need to discipline yourself in terms of –

- How much time you spend generally on Twitter
- How many people you follow – if you're new, I would start with about 20, a mix of friends, business contacts (like me), entertainers or sportspeople, journalists or other 'thinkers' …
- How many tweets you want sent direct to your phone – not too many or you will be constantly interrupted!

But overall – yes, I recommend it as a useful tool, and not just with the selfish interest of getting my own following up!

***

A Critical Look at Category Management

I come to praise category management, not bury it. Or do I mean the other way around?

No, really, category management ('CatMan') has been perhaps the most powerful sourcing tool in the procurement armoury for some years. Its launch and promulgation gave the profession a boost of credibility, and a process that enabled us to show a structured and well-thought-out approach to performing a core part of the procurement role. No longer was procurement just the Department that accepted random requisitions and placed purchase orders – we were professionals, with a proactive approach to what we were doing.

Its main impact was in the indirect spending area. Procurement in a manufacturing environment had been run on what we might call a category management basis for many years, even if we didn't call it that, probably since the beginnings of the function. I was the 'Raw Materials (EU-controlled materials)' buyer for Mars in my first functional role, then Head of Packaging Buying. We would now see those as first a fairly junior then a more senior CatMan role, but that was well before the days of consultants such as A.T. Kearney and McKinsey popularising the approach and the associated terminology.

But it was in indirect spend areas such as Marketing, MRO, IT, Facilities, Travel, Fleet, HR and Professional Services that CatMan really brought something to procurement. It gave us tools to go out to the business owners of these spend areas and say with confidence, 'We can help you do this better.'

But 20 years on from the work done by pharma company SmithKline Beecham (with McKinsey), work that certainly awakened me to 'strategic sourcing' and then category management, it is worth standing back and asking whether CatMan still deserves this central place in our professional thinking and toolbox. Has it outlived its usefulness? Does it need radical updating? Or is it still fit for purpose?

One fundamental challenge comes from what we have termed 'Market Informed Sourcing' or MIS. Others have different terms – optimisation, collaborative sourcing, advanced sourcing, and so on.

Our hypothesis is that MIS, whilst not appropriate in every case, does challenge a basic tenet of CatMan. That arises because in MIS we ask the *market* to determine how it can best meet our needs. In CatMan, the buyer generally carries out research in order to arrive at a structured approach to the market, that usually restricts greatly how suppliers can respond to our approach. Category Management closes down options; MIS opens them up.

But there are several other issues around CatMan that we do believe lead to the conclusion that we should take a fresh look at the whole topic.

1. Category Management was designed by the consulting profession and a number of the features – deliberately or fortuitously – fit the consulting model very nicely. For instance, the original design of a standardised process, combined with the need for heavy-duty data collection and analysis, played into the consultants' hands when the process was first developed and promoted.

2. That standardisation of process brings built-in weaknesses, particularly in a world that moves and changes ever faster. Is it still feasible to use a time-consuming process, with multiple steps carried out sequentially, given the need for speed in many spend areas? And is it appropriate to apply what is fundamentally the same process applied to wildly different spend areas?

3. Category Management very much placed the procurement function

and manager at the centre of the process. Suppliers were seen as almost passive players. And internal stakeholders, whilst recognised as having a role, were generally seen as being subservient to the all-powerful category manager. There are many failed CatMan programmes that bear testament to the problems with that perception.

4. Whilst most CatMan five-, seven- or nine-stage processes did – and do – recognise contract and supplier management at the back-end of that standard process, those steps were often presented as something of an afterthought. There was little doubt where the real CatMan action and focus were positioned – the research, and then most critically the approach to the market and competitive sourcing process that almost every category plan included at its heart. Yet in our view, contract and supplier management is at least as important as the upfront contracting in terms of extracting value from the contract and relationship.

So, let's explore some of these issues in more detail and suggest ways of overcoming the potential CatMan weaknesses. The first is what we might define as an overly procurement-centric approach to the whole task in hand. The buyer is placed in an almost deity-like position, controlling the whole process, with other participants fitting into their scheme and doing what they are told to by the all-powerful category manager.

Well, anyone with experience in procurement knows that life just isn't like that. And the larger and more complex the organisation is, the starker the experience will likely have been, as issues of driving change in complex organisations inevitably come to the fore. The idea that internal stakeholders would (for instance) accept major changes in strategy and supplier choice, simply because procurement decided on a new approach, was naive. In practice such changes were often simply rejected by budget holders, and the theoretical or predicted gains never materialised.

Indeed, many early programmes failed because internal stakeholders did not buy into the process or play the appropriate, and essential, role that they should have. Stakeholders need to contribute to the understanding of the category, and they need to be firmly involved in developing category plans and strategies.

That both makes the strategies better, and greatly increases the chances that those stakeholders will accept new suppliers or other changes to their supply situation. In almost every case, stakeholders also will have to play a central role in contract and supplier management if the benefits are to be captured and realised.

In one major UK programme that largely failed after a huge consulting investment, the failure was in the main down to the lack of buy-in from across a large, dispersed organisation with some very independently minded business units. Procurement and the CatMan consulting team worked on the assumption that the main source of savings would be through aggregation, by getting the organisation to standardise further on requirements, then using common strategies to leverage suppliers across business units.

But this wasn't tested with senior users and stakeholders before the programme started, and the programme was never able to communicate benefits credibly and persuade those users to give up local freedoms in return for nebulous (or at least that's how it appeared to them) corporate benefits. That ultimately caused the programme to fail despite the best efforts of skilled consultants and a capable procurement team.

Now we have seen changes here over the years – changes generally for the better. CatMan standard processes started to feature more in the way of stakeholder management tools, processes and approaches. Identifying stakeholders who are powerful and influential, both those who are positive and those who are less so, is now seen as key to successful CatMan. Techniques for influencing and persuading are more commonly discussed, and training in behavioural areas is less of the relation to technical training.

And buyers are getting some help, too. Recently we've seen impressive software that helps to ensure the CatMan process gets the right buy-in and sign-off at all stages, and tracks actions and benefits right through to bottom-line captured benefits.

But the CatMan focus on procurement was not only an issue in terms of those other internal folk who really need to be more involved. Similarly, some processes treated the supply side very much as almost passive observers of the CatMan process. And suppliers were treated the same whether they were critical strategic suppliers, or one of many in a highly tactical category.

Again, there have been some improvements in this area. Perhaps linked to growing understanding of Supplier Relationship Management and similar ideas, buyers are generally more sensitive to the need to treat suppliers appropriately depending on just what sort of relationship is desired.

So, it's important to point out that these are not insurmountable weaknesses in the CatMan process. As long as procurement understands the importance of involving other key internal players in the process – right from the beginnings of establishing requirement, right through to contract and supplier management – then their chances of success will rise considerably. And treating suppliers as more than just pawns in the CatMan game will also pay dividends – particularly where you're looking at a category with important, critical or powerful firms involved.

***

Chapter 6

FRAUD

The first article here could have been included in our last chapter, too. Indeed, quite a few of the fraud stories I wrote relate to the public sector – perhaps it's just more likely they get into the public domain than those in the private sector which tend to be hushed up, in my personal experience!

Serco Accused of Ministry of Justice Fraud

I suspect there was some midnight oil burnt in the offices of Serco last night as another public sector contracting scandal involving the firm hit the press. 'Fraudulent behaviour' has been uncovered by the Ministry of Justice in connection with Serco's contract in London and East Anglia to escort prisoners to and from courts. Apparently, Serco employees have recorded prisoners as having been delivered, when they weren't.

One worrying aspect is that this doesn't even sound like a fraud designed to enrich individuals. According to *The Guardian*,[1]

> some Serco staff were recording prisoners as having been ready for court when in fact they were not. This data is a key performance measure for the contract that could determine whether or not it is terminated …

It seems that the 'potentially fraudulent behaviour' has been going on for some time, since poor performance last year led to the Ministry telling Serco to pull their socks up. But it looks like the firm did

[1] https://www.theguardian.com/business/2013/aug/28/police-serco-alleged-fraud

not address the underlying issues, but rather just fiddled the figures.

This is serious – in a sense, if it were a few individuals doing something for personal gain, you can position it as a 'few bad apples' argument. But the perpetrators by the sound of it were acting to benefit the firm, not themselves, which suggests something more corporate in nature.

Chris Grayling, the Justice Minister, has said that 'we have not seen evidence of systemic malpractice up to board level', but how far up the management chain did this go? That's a key question.

It appears that this came to light because of the review of contracts following the recent issues around overcharging for prisoner tagging services, in which both Serco and G4S were implicated. But both customers and the Serco Board must be wondering – what else might come out? I suspect any public organisation that has contracts with Serco will be considering their own audit now. And if they're not, perhaps they should.

Serco has agreed to pay back £2 million profit on the contract to the Ministry. The FT points out that the £40m contract accounts for less than 0.9% of Serco's annual turnover, but of course the reputational damage this could do is far greater than that.

It does make you wonder how many other horror stories there are around major public sector outsourcing, and whether this drip feed of bad news will undermine public confidence in outsourcing government work in general.

And whilst it is good news for the taxpayer that this has been found now, it suggests again that contract management in the public sector needs to be strengthened. But that isn't a new thought – here's a couple of headlines (there are many more in a similar vein) from a National Audit Office report dated December 2008 on the subject:

'There are weaknesses in key performance indicators and limited use of financial incentives to drive supplier performance.'

'Central government's management of service contracts is not consistently delivering value for money.'

At the same time, a good practice framework for contract management was developed and issued, but the Office of Government Commerce never really picked up on the actions from the NAO work and until recently, Cabinet Office and ERG in this administration again didn't show much interest in contract management. Yes, I have mentioned it before, and you can probably guess why (I wrote it).

Anyway, the big question today is – do I sell the Serco shares I hold in my personal pension scheme? Or should I ride out the 10% fall we've seen this morning? *(I'm pleased to say I did sell)!*

***

The alleged Indian helicopter scandal has continued to rumble on for years – this article is from 2013.

Indian Helicopters Affair: Still Hovering Around …

There's a current revealing but disappointing example of how corruption in procurement matters can have a wider and more serious effect than might be initially apparent.

The Italian manufacturer Finmeccanica has been accused of bribing officials in the Indian Air Force to secure a $750 million deal in 2010 to sell the AW-101 medium-lift helicopters. Giuseppe Orsi, the Chairman and Chief Executive of Finmeccanica, was arrested the other week, along with Bruno Spagnolini, the Chief Executive of AgustaWestland (a Finmeccanica subsidiary) on corruption and tax fraud charges.

David Cameron, the UK's Prime Minister, said the issue of whether bribes were paid to win a contract was a matter for India and the Italian company, Finmeccanica. But it is not as simple as that – the reverberations are being felt way beyond Italy and the Indian military.

The machines would actually be made at the AgustaWestland helicopter plant in Yeovil, in the south-west of England. Hundreds of jobs are now at risk if the order is cancelled. And the British Prime Minister's trip last week to India, aimed in the main at drumming up more trade between the countries, has been negatively coloured by the whole affair.

The Indian Defence Minister A.K. Antony said that if a probe reveals proof of bribery, the Italian company and its Britain-based subsidiary 'are liable for criminal actions; they are liable to be prosecuted; the company is liable to be blacklisted'.

Military equipment is one of the UK's export success stories, but there have been previous allegations (and more definite cases) of corruption involving a number of firms and trading partners. But this looks like it might have particularly serious implications beyond the immediate participants.

There are also implications in India. The country needs to update its military arsenal, but defence procurement is well known for its extreme slowness. 10 years is not unusual for a contracting process! (And Francis Maude worries about nine months in the UK …) So, as well as the concern for jobs in the UK, this could lead to further paralysis in India, in terms of major military and perhaps other government procurement.

All this shows that while we might get frustrated with certain aspects of public procurement rules and regulations, the effect of breaking those rules, particularly in cases involving bribery and corruption, can have hugely negative effects. As indeed do similar events in the private sector, even if they rarely break into the public view.

So, whilst we can never eliminate problems, in both public and private sectors, there are precautions that can help. Robust, clear procurement processes, automation to help with transparency and audit trail, and skilled, capable individuals are all bulwarks against the risk of corruption.

***

This may have been the first time I wrote about 'invoice misdirection' fraud, but it didn't and hasn't gone away. It is simple but seems to be very effective.

Olympic Invoicing Fraud – Is Your Organisation Vulnerable?

We've asked this before – is procurement (in its widest sense) fraud on the increase? Is it driven in part by economic pressures, and perhaps also by the general feeling that 'everyone is in it for themselves', whether that is politicians, premiership footballers or bankers? So why shouldn't I take what I believe I 'deserve' when I see everyone else apparently doing the same?

Whether or not it is increasing, there was another interesting example in the press last week. The UK Olympic Delivery Authority (ODA) and the construction firm Skanska were the victims of what appears to be a fairly simple but elegant fraud. The fraudster contacted the ODA at a time when a large invoice payment was due to Skanska. As the BBC reported:

191

'He obtained the £2.3m by pretending to be Skanska's finance director and writing to the ODA with a change of account details ahead of a bank transfer. The account details he gave were his own.'

Pretty damn simple really.

Given that the ODA said 95% of the money had been 'recovered', one assumes that the ODA did actually make the payments. It was always going to be discovered of course – a short time later, one assumes Skanska called the ODA and said, 'Oi, where's our dosh?' Or the equivalent in Swedish.

At which point, after some desperate tracking down of payment details, all would become clear. It seems that the fraudsters relied on covering their tracks by the time it was discovered, and they had worked out a fascinating money laundering route, whereby the money would go off to Nigeria, but would then be used to 'buy a parade of shops in Wolverhampton'.

Now, let's take a short detour from the serious point here. If I had successfully got away with a couple of million, I can think of a few things I might do / buy. Luxury hotels, champagne, and expensive gifts for a certain member of the GB cycling team might even come into it. (No, not Sir Chris Hoy.)

But I have to say, a parade of shops in Wolverhampton wouldn't be high on my list! Oh well, each to their own, as they say.

But what can we learn from this? Well, flippancy aside, it confirms how vital it is to have accurate supplier data, and robust processes around seemingly mundane issues such as recording of bank details. It doesn't say much obviously for the ODA's processes in this area, although they say: 'Our payments system was reviewed and strengthened immediately after the incident to further limit the risk of fraud.'

It's also interesting to speculate that if ODA and Skanska had been able to communicate very quickly and easily, a rapid check would have discovered the fraud before money changed hands.

That's another potential benefit from the trend towards more collaborative 'social media'-type links between buyer and seller that we're seeing – firms from Tradeshift to Wax Digital, Rollstream to SAP are all looking to make that communication much more natural. So, a quick tweet or Facebook wall-type communication from ODA, via a collaborative supplier platform, to the contact in Skanska saying, 'Hi, Sue, can you confirm you've changed your bank details?' would have stopped this in its tracks.

But whatever your current systems and processes, it's worth looking at whether your organisation would be vulnerable to something as simple but effective as this fraud.

***

It isn't only the public sector that suffers from fraud, although it is rare for such an interesting private sector case as this one to reach the courts.

Sainsbury's Potato Fraud Hits the Courts

As one fraud case reached its conclusion, when Ross Knowles, energy buying chief from Kent County Council's LASER collaborative buying organisation, was sent down for seven years, another hit the courts.

John Maylam, the Sainsbury's potato buyer, pleaded guilty to demanding bribes from Greenvale AP in return for awarding them valuable potato supply contracts. The bribes were then funded by Sainsbury's paying Greenvale slightly over the odds, for lots and lots of potatoes.

One technique was to add on one pound to the price of a crate, and with the volume we are talking about, it soon adds up. The supplier also supplied smaller packs for the same price and there were 'illogical prices' for new packs.

Greenvale secured a £40 million contract and opened an account called 'The Fund' into which they paid £8.7 million of Sainsbury's money, giving £4.9 million to Maylam, 44, and his associates and keeping the rest for themselves. Maylam also allegedly ran up a £200,000 bill at Claridge's hotel in London and enjoyed a £350,000 trip to Monaco with the cash given to him over two years by Baxter, the Greenvale account manager.

Maylam admitted corruption when he appeared before Croydon Crown Court in South London last week. Baxter pleaded guilty to giving him the payments. They'll be sentenced after the trial of Greenvale finance director Andrew Behagg, who denies corruption.

It's interesting that, according to the report[2] when the arrests were first made back in 2008, the fraud wasn't discovered by Sainsbury's. It was auditors from the parent company of Greenvale who spotted unusual payments and blew the whistle.

> Following an internal investigation by Produce Investments Ltd, the holding company for Greenvale AP, the matter of payments made to individuals outside the Produce Investments group was brought to the attention of J Sainsbury plc.

Scams like this are one of the most difficult types of procurement-related fraud to uncover. That may be why it has taken four years to put the evidence together. I'm convinced that collusion between buyer and seller is very common; and where suppliers are paying bribes, they are likely to recover that 'investment' in some manner by mechanisms such as higher prices.

---

[2] http://www.telegraph.co.uk/news/uknews/1581837/Sainsburys-potato-buyer-arrested-in-3m-bribe-case.html

How can organisations guard against this type of fraud, then? Three immediate options come to mind.

1. Don't keep procurement people in the same job for too long – as well as the almost inevitable complacency, opportunities for fraud grow as people on each side of the negotiating table get to know each other better.

2. Don't allow all the power and knowledge to be concentrated. Why didn't someone else spot that the prices being paid were above the market? An assistant, a peer, a boss, someone who could say, 'Hang on, why are we buying so much from Greenvale when they're expensive?'

3. Price benchmarking is a powerful tool both to ensure competitiveness and to guard against fraud. It's surprising Sainsbury's didn't have some sort of process in place given the competitive nature of the supermarket world.

4. Finally, and perhaps the most powerful option, open, transparent procurement processes with a clear audit trail make this sort of fraud much more difficult. If there has been an e-sourcing process, or even an e-auction perhaps, where the various bids were recorded, it would have been difficult for Maylam to show favour without an objective reason; or for the supplier to load the prices.

And well done to the *Daily Mirror*, for the headline of the day – 'For Mash, Get Cash!'

***

Finally, in terms of case studies, one of the most shocking frauds I've ever seen, a case that may well have cost lives.

Fraudster's Useless 'Bomb Detection' Kit Sends Him to Jail

A fraudster was found guilty this week after selling millions of pounds' worth of 'bomb detection kits' that turned out to be totally ineffective. Indeed, they appear to have been little more than a car aerial and some bits of plastic, and were modelled on novelty golf ball finders. The antenna was 'no more a radio antenna than a nine-inch nail', according to one scientist.

Yet over £50 million worth were sold, many in Iraq, which, goodness knows, could have done with some real bomb detection. He even got some help from government, whilst whistleblowers were ignored by politicians to whom they expressed their concern. Here's The Guardian:[33]

> Jim McCormick, 57, who was convicted at the Old Bailey on Tuesday of three counts of fraud, was trained at a 'how to sell to the UN' seminar organised by UK Trade and Industry in March 2008. He also held meetings with officials at UK Trade & Investment, the export-promotion arm of the Department for Business.

The question for anyone looking at this, and perhaps even more so for procurement people, is how on earth he got away with it for so long? Why weren't the products tested properly? – it can't be that difficult to see whether a piece of equipment can actually detect

[3] https://www.theguardian.com/uk/2013/apr/23/uk-government-helped-fake-bomb-detector-fraudster

explosives. Amazingly, the equipment was still being used in some places even as McCormick stood trial.

The answer appears to be simple. The buying decisions weren't made on rational, objective grounds. They were often made by people who were being bribed to buy the kit, people who didn't care about its effectiveness, but did care about the chance to make their own fortunes in a country beset by uncertainty and fear. For instance, General Jihad al-Jabiri, who ran the Baghdad bomb squad, is in prison on corruption charges relating to the contracts. Others were misled by fake demonstrations of the product, and just didn't look hard enough at its real worth. They may have wanted to believe it would work – a magic solution to a big problem.

So next time we moan about European public sector procurement processes, rules and bureaucracy, or complain about how long it takes to get things done in government, just remember – that is a price we pay to make as sure as possible we don't have episodes like this.

But don't think 'it couldn't happen here'. We wrote recently about the conflicts of interest emerging in UK health commissioning, and there is a certain percentage of people who, if they see the opportunity to make money corruptly, with little chance of detection, will take it. So, we need to keep our guard up at all times. And even with all our precautions, we can be sure that someone, somewhere, is carrying out a procurement-related fraud in the UK public sector right now.

It probably won't be based on dodgy bomb-detection equipment, however.

***

Moving on from specific fraud cases, I wrote about the difficulty of detecting it, and gave some thoughts on why procurement fraud happens, as well as some tips for avoiding it.

'How Dare You!?' Chris Huhne Pleads Guilty

If I accused you of committing fraud or of acting corruptly in your role as a procurement professional (or indeed whatever role you currently fill), how would you react?

I suspect you would be angry. You might shout at me, or worse. You might be indignant – how dare you accuse me of these sins or crimes? You would be hurt. Me? You really think I'm the sort of person who would do that?

You could even become threatening. I'll sue you for slander. I'll get you back – you haven't heard the end of this.

All of these emotions and responses are totally understandable. That's certainly how I expect I would react in a similar situation. Now, let's imagine that I'm accusing someone who, it turns out, really *has* been committing fraud. How might they react?

You see the problem? Their reaction is likely to be exactly the same as that of the totally innocent, wrongly accused individual. They may be dissembling, rather than expressing genuine emotion, but they are likely to make the same responses.

How dare you! I'm very upset by the accusation. I've been loyal to this firm for 20 years. If you repeat this to anyone, you'll hear from my lawyer!

And they'll keep going on that tack, right up to the moment when they realise they've been found out, at which point their whole approach will change. Then they usually seek to admit some blame, but mitigate the seriousness of the offence.

We've seen two classic cases recently. Cyclist Lance Armstrong went as far as suing journalists (successfully) who claimed he was taking drugs and calling a woman who tried to expose him a 'whore'. That needs remembering, however much some call for his rehabilitation.

And now Chris Huhne, the UK politician, has pleaded guilty to perverting the course of justice, after getting his wife to accept a speeding conviction on his behalf. He vigorously denied everything. 'I'm innocent of these charges,' he announced to the cameras a year ago. He kept on making protestations of innocence – right up to the moment he pleaded guilty in court.

So, two messages here for procurement. Firstly, you need to be on very firm ground before making accusations about fraud (or anything else). People don't usually go, 'It's a fair cop,' at the first mention of problems. And rather than getting into that uncomfortable position of having to accuse someone (and it is deeply uncomfortable), it's a lot better to cut off the possibility at source.

That means having the right procurement policies, processes and practices in place to make it very difficult for people to do the wrong things, and to improve the chances of detection if and when fraud does occur. It's impossible to remove the risk completely, but we can make it less likely.

***

Why Does Fraud Happen?

While I'm not a huge fan of the modern detective novel, between the ages of 14 and 16, I read everything Agatha Christie and Raymond Chandler ever wrote. And if I remember one thing about crime, it's this:

MOTIVE + OPPORTUNITY = BAD THINGS HAPPEN

Fraud is a crime, and the same equation works for a manager falsifying invoices to a dummy company, just as it does for the jealous wife with an unfaithful husband, a life assurance policy on his head, and a penchant for admiring the view over the hotel balcony ...

So, everyone who commits fraud has a motive. Now we might consider that those motives are hard to legislate against in the business environment. But an understanding of motivation might help organisations spot where risk may be greater and take preemptive actions to reduce the chance of that potential turning into money disappearing out of the door (or the bank account).

My hypothesis is that there are three key reasons (motives) why people – particularly internal staff – commit fraud. In no particular order:

Financial need – the most obvious, often driven by a problem such as debt. That may be caused by factors outside their control, such as mortgage rate increases, or more avoidable drivers such as a liking for expensive company of the opposite sex. Gambling is another not unusual factor that leads to debt and ultimately crime. In one case I'm aware of, a senior accountant made payments to a dummy supplier (which he controlled) because he had 'the Peterborough* ⁴mafia' on his back for greyhound racing betting debts.

A *psychological defect* (as we might call it) – perhaps a pathological desire for excitement; or a 'cry for help', as the newspapers like to put it. This is often unrelated to a tangible need for cash and doesn't appear to be even simple greed – there's a parallel perhaps

---

* A mid-sized city in Eastern England, once an agricultural / religious centre, now a light industry / services hub. And apparently popular with illegal gambling rings...

with the shoplifting habits of Hollywood stars like Winona Ryder. In another case, I know of two very senior marketing executives who were fired for a complex fraud involving submitting duplicated hotel bills to generate expense claims. Given the return compared to their salaries, I suspect it was driven by the thrill of the fraud, rather than real financial need.

A sense that *'I deserve it'* – whilst this could be considered as pure greed, it is often driven by a feeling of being undervalued in their job, or a jealousy of others. Perpetrators may even feel they are morally in the clear, and academic research suggests this is a major driver of fraud. It's often evident in the type of fraud where a secretary or administrator working for a very rich individual, or a junior person in a firm where top staff are highly rewarded, helps themselves to some of the boss's wealth.

This final factor interests me. As the gap between rich and poor gets wider in our societies, are more people feeling like this? When a mid-level executive, whose salary is fairly static (or worse) sees bankers and CEOs earning millions, and footballers, rockstars or baseball players rewarded handsomely, are they more likely to think, 'Why not me? – I deserve it as much as him / her.'?

Clearly, the first of our three factors – financial need – is likely to become more significant in tough economic times. Whether or not the final factor changes over time, I don't know for certain, but it seems likely as inequality grows generally. So, we can assume, I suggest, that two of the key motivational drivers for fraud are increasing.

Is there anything organisations can do to counter this? Should organisations try to identify addictive personalities, or those individuals who are intrinsically thrill seeking? Avoiding blatantly unfair allocation of reward is clearly sensible for many reasons, not merely in order to minimise the chances of fraud. Being aware of staff who may feel, rightly or wrongly, that they're undervalued, and not putting them in a position with the potential for fraud, is sensible.

But perhaps it's just a case of being aware that fraud does happen, and the drivers, and keeping alert to individuals' behaviour that might suggest a tendency to fall into one of these categories. But more importantly, process and control measures can be put in place to reduce that opportunity of fraud, whatever the motivation.

***

Six Anti-Fraud Measures

How can organisations stop procurement-related fraud, or at least make it as difficult as possible?

While there is a wide variety of frauds, there are a relatively small number of key principles that, if understood and acted upon properly, can make fraud at least more difficult. (It is never impossible!) Some of the principles also make it more likely that fraud is detected, even if it hasn't been cut off at source.

Fraud relies on extracting money from the organisation, either in return for nothing, or in return for less value than the money justifies. So, the basic counter-fraud principles must be around controlling the flow of money out of the organisation, and ensuring that full value has been obtained for that money.

But as well as the key principles, there is also an overarching need to codify the processes and the policies that are in force and followed in the organisation. They should cover how procurement is executed; for instance, how a Procurement Card should be used, or the flow of requisitions and orders. These policies are the key 'rules' – so everything from the need to declare conflict of interest, to when a single tender can be used, to sign-off limits on invoices.

We'll now describe broadly each principle and what needs to be done – but we are not going to get into the full implications, or, for instance, the technology that might be used to counter fraudulent activities.

1. It must be clear who is entitled to spend money in the organisation.
A basic principle, yet one that often isn't followed. Only certain people in an organisation should be allowed to commit the organisation's money to third parties. That doesn't mean of course that they will do it well or properly, but by restricting the number we do at least reduce the overall field of potential fraudsters. Clarity in this area also makes it more difficult for the fraudster who is discovered to say, 'I didn't know I wasn't allowed to do it like this.' It is also important to clarify the difference between a budget holder – who has accountability for expenditure generally – and a procurement authority – someone who can agree contracts with third parties. They may be one and the same person, but that is not necessarily so.

2. Any expenditure committed must be authorised properly.
The first and most basic precaution against fraud should be the check on what is being committed to a third party. Does the commitment look appropriate? Are the goods or services the sorts of things we would expect to see the organisation ordering? Does the supplier look genuine? Is the commitment within the individual's authority levels? These are the sorts of questions that should be considered by the authoriser of the expenditure.

We often see a temptation to allow more senior managers to place orders without any further authorisation. Apart from very low-value orders, we do not consider this good practice. Evidence suggests that it is often middle and senior executives who commit fraud, which is simply a case of those being the people who have the opportunity to do so. It is not an insult to ask a director to have their expenditure authorised; it is good practice at any level of the organisation.

3. All entities to which money is paid must be verified and authorised.
The principle above gives a basic sense-check of an order. But how do we know that order isn't going to a dummy company, controlled by the order placer (the fraudster) or their associates? That 'supplier' may still supply the goods and services required, or something approximating them, with the fraud being the nature / quality or quantity of what is provided. Or they may supply nothing, relying on no one other than the fraudster realising this, or on a time lag which gives everyone, including the internal fraudster, the chance to safely disappear before anyone says, 'Where are those 5000 laptops that we ordered (and paid for)?'

So, checking that the entity to whom orders are placed and / or money is paid is genuine is key. Are they a genuine company with a trading history? Do they have a track record? Who are the directors? This is clearly an area where appropriate supplier information management processes, systems and tools absolutely come into their own.

4. Procured goods or services must be checked to ensure that what was received (quality, quantity etc.) is aligned with the contract and payment.
Even if we see that the requirement is genuine, and the supplier is genuine, fraud can take place where the nature of what is supplied – quality, quantity, specification – is not as contracted for. So, a lower-

value product is substituted if we are talking about goods. Or in the case of services, it may be the quantity that is the heart of the fraud.

Perhaps the most difficult procurement fraud to detect would be a budget holder and a professional services supplier in collusion, with the budget holder signing off that 20 days of consulting or contingent labour services were provided when really it was only 15. This is very difficult to detect; but some additional checks on what has really been received, obviously involving more than just the single budget holder, provide some protection here.

5. Supplier selection and pricing of purchased goods and services must be transparent.
Even if the goods or services received are as per the contract, how do we know the price paid was appropriate? And even if the price was reasonable, are we sure the supplier was selected in a fair and transparent manner, rather than because of a bribe or connection to the buyer? This, like the previous example, is very hard to detect. Perhaps the manager paying £1,000 a day for a contractor should only be paying the market price of £800. The senior manager may be taking the £200 'excess' back as a bribe for awarding the contractor the work. Transparency over selection decisions and value for money can at least reduce the risk of this particular fraud.

6. Opportunities for collusion between suppliers, and between suppliers and buyers, must be minimised.
Many of the frauds we've described rely on collusion between buyer or budget holder and seller. So, reducing the chances of this will reduce the chance of fraud. Steps can be taken to ensure that there is always more than one person involved with any major procurement or in signing-off work with suppliers. Moving staff regularly is another option, so there is less time for the relationship, and perhaps

the fraudulent plans, to mature. Some organisations have a policy that no one in a decision-making procurement role will stay for more than three years in that same job role for this reason.

It is not just procurement people of course to whom this applies. Indeed, procurement often worries about stakeholders (budget holders, users) getting too close to suppliers. It may be very innocent, but when the marketing or IT manager makes it clear that (s)he doesn't want procurement involved with 'their' relationship with a key supplier – that can be a warning sign that it isn't totally innocent. Organisations should look at discouraging closeness that goes beyond the need to work well with a supplier to get a job done. This may influence, for instance, the policy on hospitality and entertainment.

We could say a lot more – but if you act on the principles we've outlined here, you will at the very least reduce the chances of successful procurement fraud going on in your organisation.

**

CHAPTER 7

CEREBRAL WHIMSY

One of the nicest comments I got about my work was from legendary procurement guru, Dr Dick Russill. He called my writing 'A surreal mix of hardcore procurement and cerebral whimsy', hence the title of this chapter. Just occasionally, it is fun to look at procurement with a humorous lens. So here are a few examples of that, along with a diversion into my gambling problem …

A Seasonal Case Study

'Oh yes,' he laughs, as Father Christmas and I enjoy a cocktail at one of London's finest hotels. 'I remember when I would have been in a state of panic at this time! 8pm on Christmas Eve. Worrying about whether I'd got everything, and how the reindeer would stand up to the exertions of the evening. Now frankly I can just sit back and enjoy myself.'

I was there to present FC – as he insisted I called him – with his Supply Chain Innovation award on behalf of the global procurement and supply chain community. 'I think the first step was when we sat down and worked out a clear make-buy strategy. What we would manufacture ourselves, and what we would buy in (direct from the manufacturer whatever possible). Then we looked at the in-house manufacturing requirement and took the difficult decision to offshore much of it. Nothing wrong with elves, lovely guys, but the work ethic … not a patch on certain emerging countries, you know. Took 30% out of the cost base.'

He continued, after another sip of his piña colada. 'In terms of what we buy in, we determined where we could use e-sourcing and auctions. Where requirements were complex we use very smart optimisation platforms to look at different options: buying in final products or buying subcomponents and contracting for assembly, for instance. We've also used optimisation for some of the logistics, whether we ask for delivery to the North Pole or our new regional hubs, for instance.

But where we're buying branded goods, auctions are less effective. So there's still a role for negotiation, but we use cost-modelling and supply chain analysis to make sure we're on the front foot. And it is amazing how well the reindeer have responded to retraining. There are a few sales people who've made pretty big price concessions when they're faced with a metre-long set of antlers across the negotiating table!'

Before all of that we have to understand the requirements. We pick up the children's lists now from Amazon wish lists and similar – much easier than re-constructing those burnt bits of paper! Then we use some smart spend analytics-type software to develop a global 'present cube' which we can interrogate by product, region, cost etc. Essential when it comes to both our sourcing and our logistics planning.'

What about the transactional side of things?

'Yes, our P2P (pixie-to-pixie) processes are very effective now. We've moved beyond electronic invoicing to magic invoicing – I just think of a number and it is automatically paid into the supplier's bank account. I'm licencing the technology to Ariba and Basware next year, so look out for it on the market!

And we've started promoting supply chain finance. With my infinite resources, I'm a pretty attractive customer, so we're using that to help our suppliers and get some even better deals ourselves.

Some of our suppliers weren't happy being paid with Santa's Magic Coins, but with the dollar and the euro looking weak, increasingly it is being seen as a good option. I fact, we hear that some big corporates might issue SMC-denominated bonds next year!'

Does corporate social responsibility feature in FC's thinking now?

'Absolutely. We use various tools and information providers to track and analyse our supply base and individual suppliers. We try and support smaller and minority-owned businesses; we've been particularly active this year with leprechaun- and nymph-owned businesses because of the problems in their countries.'

And finally, what about the controversial decision to stop reindeer-based deliveries? FC is unrepentant.

'Bad for the environment, bad for the reindeer, bad for the customers. You've no idea how much methane reindeer produce over a busy night's flying. Since we've outsourced to Amazon, DHL, TNT and FedEx things have improved significantly.'

***

Newspaper reports suggested that the UK and its oldest friend and oldest enemy, France, might work together on a new aircraft carrier programme. Really??

Top Secret – Anglo-French Aircraft Carrier Meeting Minutes

We have just obtained a copy of a secret document from sources in Whitehall, and despite great personal risk, we have decided it is in the public interest to publish it.

Notes from the first meeting of the Anglo-French Aircraft Carrier Strategy and Design Committee

Present:
Admiral Sir Archibald Nelson-Mountbatten (2nd Sea Lord) (ANM)
William Hudson, GCMG (Ministry of Defence) (WH)
Admiral Napoleon Marquis de Sade de Carrefour (French Navy) (NMSC)
François Le Clerc (Ministère de la Défense) (FL)

FL opened the meeting with traditional French fraternal greetings ('où est le stylo de ma tante?')

WH responded, 'Sur le pont d'Avignon.'

ANM called 'Heads' successfully, so once FL had inspected the coin, the meeting was held in English.

ANM said he was very happy to be discussing this collaboration.

FL said that 'collaboration' was not the best word to use perhaps with the French military leadership. 'Co-operation' had fewer unpleasant historical resonances in France.

NMSC said there were a few things he needed to get on the table. Notably, that the lunch break was a non-negotiable three hours, and wine would be served at every meal including breakfast. He was also worried that now female ratings were part of the ship's company, clearly the British sailors wouldn't get a look in with all the handsome French sailors around. Although from what he had heard, maybe les Anglais weren't all that interested in the ladies, si vous savez what I mean?

ANM's response has been struck from the records. There was then a long discussion about the recreational facilities to be provided. A multipurpose boules and croquet pitch was agreed as a good compromise.

WH commented it was a good job the Spanish weren't involved, we'd have to build a bullring on the aft deck.

The likely mobilisation of the ship was discussed. FL said he couldn't really see it going any further than Marseilles, not much point really, maybe have a little sail around the Med in September, nice that time of year.

ANM stressed the need to provide South Atlantic and possibly Antarctic capability. NMSC said he couldn't really see his men putting up with all that cold; it was only a few stupid islands anyway.

ANM's comment has been struck from the records.

It was agreed that the ship should have some guns. Big guns were very much preferred if there was any money left after building the ship.

WH stressed that the contracts for construction would have to be let in a fair and transparent manner. FL said he agreed: his procurement team in Paris was already working on it, and it would be let in exactly the same manner as all other French military contracts. He was confident that British suppliers would have an excellent chance of winning the business. NMSC appeared to have a coughing fit at this point.

Unfortunately, the project was deemed cancelled after agreement could not be reached on two key points:

A. Whether the planes would take off / land from the starboard or port side?
B. Left or right-hand drive?

The meeting was cordially terminated at 12 noon precisely (pour le déjeuner).

***

When the CIPS (the Chartered Institute of Procurement and Supply) announced that their aim was to establish a situation where everyone who was a buyer for their organisation would need to have a CIPS licence, it was a great opportunity for us to have fun with the idea. Here are two examples.

Deadlier than Crack? The Latest Addiction Hits the UK

Following a campaign by the Chartered Institute of Purchasing and Supply, everyone who buys on behalf of their organisation has to be formally licenced. But tonight, on Spend Matters Tough Talk, we look at the growing problem of individuals – often in good, responsible jobs – whose terrible addiction means they're falling foul of this new law and ruining their lives.

Our reporter spoke to one of the victims. He asked to remain anonymous, so we got him to wear a silly wig and a false nose.

So, Jim, how did it start?

Well, I was just a normal bloke really. Decent job, running a small department, nice firm, you know. Kept my nose clean, decent salary, no problems. Then one day – I can remember it like yesterday. But, to begin with, it was only the soft stuff ...

The soft stuff?

Yeah, copier paper. A few envelopes. We'd run out, you see. I knew I should order it from the procurement team, but I was in a hurry, I was out for a sandwich at lunchtime and – I just saw it in the newsagent, copier paper on special offer £4.99 a pack, and ... I was weak, I know. Before I knew it, I'd bought it. Brought it back to the office and used it. God, it was good. Avoiding all that paperwork, requisitions, invoices to authorise. I just put it on my expenses, and that was it. And I got away with it!

But then things got worse?

Yeah, you always think you can stop buying, but it makes you feel invincible. I did some more paper-based stationery but you know, they say it's a gateway purchase. It leads onto the hard stuff.

You say 'the hard stuff' – what sort of thing?

Furniture first of all – I bought a new chair for the office, only cheap, mind you: the old one was broken. Then some software – all stuff I really needed, I never wasted money. But I knew I was getting a kick out of it. The thrill of handing over the cash, that adrenalin high, wondering if anyone has seen my going into the store. But you have to do more and more to get that same kick. So… I started on Amazon.

That's the most addictive, isn't it?

Yeah, it's just so easy. It just gives you everything you want to buy. Everything you want. Books, software, stationery, coffee … And one click! It's like they want you to buy it! And it feels great! Soon I was doing it pretty much every day.

And then what happened?

I guess deep down I knew it couldn't last. One day my boss came into the office. I could see it on her face – she looked worse than I did. And she had one of them with her – one of those PLANCs. The Procurement Licensing and Notification Commission. The Buying Police, we call them.

I didn't make a fuss. No point really – he had the evidence, the invoices, some CCTV footage from the florist showing me buying a bunch of flowers for Susan's retirement do, that sort of thing.

He wasn't aggressive or anything. Just asked, have you got a purchasing licence? Well, we all knew the answer to that, didn't we?

So what are you doing now?

Well, I'm serving my time. My wife's stood by me, bless her heart. And they're good in here, they give me support, you know, if they see me hanging around the kitchen with a pad of requisitions in my hand when the food supplier is about to deliver, they'll calm me down, get me back to the cell. Give me the medicine.

And when you get out?

Well, you know, it might sound a bit weird, but I might actually train as a buyer. Get licenced. Do it properly. I mean, I always thought I had the aptitude.

Jim, thanks very much and good luck.

Yeah, thanks … Um, you haven't got a stapler you could sell me, have you? I've got a draft contract here. Very reasonable Ts and Cs …

Jim, you know we agreed, I can't help you. OK look, just one pencil …

***

James Pond, Licenced to … Buy?

James strolled into the casino, immaculate as ever in his Marks & Spencer's Autograph range, light grey, low-maintenance drip-dry suit (42 short) and easy-iron white shirt.

It was early, and the high rollers were thin on the ground, but James noticed everything as he strolled to the roulette table. That was his training kicking in. The thin woman in the red dress, maybe just a little too short for her age. The guy by the bar, already hitting the doubles as he also hit on the dyed blonde behind the bar.

As he sat down by the Impair – always his favourite – the croupier smiled. 'Good afternoon, m'sieur,' she purred in a deep French accent. The red hair and figure were top-class, but James could see sadness behind the eyes. He knew how she felt. Too many late nights, not enough fresh air, the wrong sort of men. Just like working in Easton on the Hill, James thought.

'Hello,' said James. 'I need to ask you a few questions.' The girl looked surprised. 'Go ahead, monsieur,' she whispered, in a voice like liquid honey and bourbon. James blushed slightly.

'I'm Pond. James Pond. Licenced to bill. Well, licenced to buy really, but billing sort of goes with buying, and licenced to bill has a ring to it, know what I mean?' The redhead looked confused. OK, thought James, let's get down to it.

'Who buys the wheels?' Now her expression was confusion, mingling deliciously with a small shot of fear.

'No one buys the wheels. We're a clean house.'

'No, I'm not talking about cheating, I mean who actually buys the roulette wheels. The purchasing. Who does the buying for the casino?'

She looked blank. James sighed. This always happened, as soon as he walked into a place, it seemed that no one knew who bought anything.

'I don't know. Perhaps we didn't buy them. Perhaps we just found them.'

The same old lies. James put his hand on her arm.

'I think you might find it to your advantage to tell me,' he said, with that hint of menace in his voice that had proved so vital during the 2007 Rail Franchising Incident.

Before the girl could answer, James was aware of a presence, like a ghost smelling of Givenchy, materialising at his left shoulder.

'Is there something wrong, Mr Bond? I'm the manager here,' the slim Italian with the slick hair and the slicker suit hissed, through a smile as fake as the barmaid's suntan.

'It's Pond, actually, not Bond.'

'Perhaps I can get you a drink and we can sort this out, Mr Pond. A dry martini, I assume?'

'I can't drink on duty, I'm afraid. But a cup of tea would be very nice. Two sugars please. Shaken not stirred.'

The Italian returned with a plastic cup filled with a pale brown liquid. Pond sniffed it suspiciously. 'Ah, that's lovely,' he said. 'Just like Mother used to make. Anyway, sorry to bother you, but I'm from the Commission.'

'The Commission? You don't mean …'

'Yes, I'm afraid you've been chosen for a random inspection by PLANC. The Purchasing Licensing and Notification Commission. We check that everyone who is carrying out buying activities in organisations is properly licenced. I'm afraid I need to know who does your buying.'

The Italian smiled. 'That would be Luigi.'

Hearing his name, a man elevated himself from a bar stool and crossed the room towards James. Around 6 foot 7, bald, heavy-set, but light on his feet. James had met his sort before, but this was never easy, he thought. Some days he longed for that transfer back to the Department for Work and Pensions, HR Policy Branch.

'This is Luigi. He does our buying.'

'Yeah, that's right, boss. I do the buying. Everything.'

'So, Luigi.' James smiled to himself. He always enjoyed this bit. 'Can you tell me how you would apply the Kraljic Matrix to assess the key areas of supply chain risk for the casino?'

The blood drained from Luigi's face.

'I don't think we covered that in the CIPS training,' he said weakly.

'Can I see your licence please?

Now Luigi smiled, exposing enough gold to stock the Tiffany's catalogue.

'Sure, here it is. CIPS, 1997. All the exams. First time, too. And I got the continuous professional development stamp on the back. Just like dose guys in Stamford say. We like to keep everythin' nice here. We don't want to offend no one, not the CIPS heavies, not PLANC.'

James took the card. Something wasn't quite right. He took a small implement out of his inside pocket.

'The latest from Q, back in the office. Detects forgeries through the latest Bayesian neuro-probability Higgs boson mesa-detection nanowave analysis.' He shone the small, torch-like device at Luigi's card.

After a few seconds, James looked up.

'I'm sorry. This is your library card.'

It all happened so quickly. Luigi reached into his jacket pocket, but before he could pull out his gun, James had his own weapon in his hand. He grabbed Luigi's shooting hand and forced it across his neck, whilst twisting Luigi's other arm behind his back. That left James with his own gun trained on the manager.

'Don't make me do anything we'll all regret. You ...' (He nodded towards the redhead.) Get over here. Go through their pockets. Weapons on the table where I can see them. And don't try anything funny or your friends will be cashing in their chips for the last time.' I know, thought James, I've used that one before. But it's good.

The girl, eyes wide, took two weapons from the manager's jacket and picked up the one Luigi had dropped. 'On the floor!' James shouted. Luigi and the manager lay down, hands behind their heads.

'OK,' said James. 'This is what is going to happen now.'

'I'm filling in Form S-27 Part 3 ProcB/187Q in triplicate – I'll leave one copy with you now. You will receive official notification in the post that you have broken PLANC licencing regulations. There is a statutory fine of £250 and you have 90 days to either get Luigi-licenced – properly – or find another licenced buyer to carry out your procurement. If you do not do that, the second fine will be £2,500 with the possibility of a 3-month prison sentence. OK?'

The guys on the floor nodded as best they could.

'Oh, I almost forgot. You have the right to appeal against the decision within the next 30 days. But honestly – don't even think about it, punks.'

James turned and walked towards the door. He hesitated for a moment, then turned back towards the croupier. 'Do you fancy a quick Starbucks? I've got a voucher for a free hazelnut muffin.'

The redhead smiled and nodded. 'That'ud be canny good, pet. I need the netty, though, ah'm bustin', but ah won't be a minute, like. Ah'll see you doonstairs.'

Perhaps it wasn't going to be just another routine day after all, thought James.

***

External events of various types provided inspiration for a bit of humour. The Ryder Cup (a golf tournament) was held in Scotland.

Supply Opportunities – Ryder Cup Coming Soon

We were excited to see that contracts for golf's 2014 Ryder Cup, to be held in Scotland, at Gleneagles, will be advertised soon. As *The Scotsman* website reported:

2014 Ryder Cup organisers are inviting businesses to tender for supplier contracts. Ryder Cup Europe expects the event at Gleneagles to employ 5,000 people directly, with many more likely to benefit through the supply chain.

The procurement portal will be hosted on the Public Contracts Scotland (PCS) website and will include opportunities including catering, merchandising, security and transport. The first contracts should be awarded within three months.

Edward Kitson, match director for the tournament, said: 'The Ryder Cup is one of the world's most prestigious events and we are looking for suppliers whose products and services will enable us to create a truly memorable occasion. The portal is a joint initiative between Ryder Cup Europe, the Scottish Government and Scottish Enterprise. It is the first time that a series of private contracts will be available through PCS.

Now – exclusive to Spend Matters – we've been given a sneak preview of some of the categories that will be advertised on the portal.

Tents – must be designed to stand 80-mile-an-hour, gale-force winds, torrential rain, sleet and snow, lightning conductors essential. Must have room for many, many bars.

Portable toilets – see above. Particularly the wind.

Security services – approximately 200 ageing gentlemen, tweed jackets compulsory, moustache preferred, to stand around greens and hold up signs saying 'Quiet'. Must NOT be tempted (difficult though that is) to shout, 'Shut up, you idiot Yank, with your stupid cries of "in the hole" when someone tees off on a 560-yard par five!'

Balls – lots of golf balls. Must be round with dimples.

Team partners' hosting services – individuals required to escort approximately 15 American ladies, aged 25-50, on a number of trips to exciting Scottish venues including shops, spas, castles (centrally heated only).

Strict checks will be carried out – anyone who is attracted to blonde, immaculately groomed, tanned, perfect-toothed women of a certain age should NOT apply. We don't want any diplomatic incidents here or someone being chased around the car park by a golfer with a three wood in hand …

Catering – you know, some Scottish delicacies, haggis and neeps, plus some stuff that people might actually eat.

Anecdote writer – approximately 150 assorted anecdotes required, Peter Alliss for the use of. Not more than 50 should start, 'and best wishes to (insert name here) who hasn't been feeling too good recently, but you'll be up and back to 36 holes a day in no time, I'm sure.' Following topics must be covered – references to the light playing on the loch, ducklings, sleeping spectators, Ian Poulter's trousers, what a great job the greenkeepers have done.

***

I've always been a Doctor Who *fan, and what a procurement opportunity this would be!*

Strategic Procurement Review of Time-Travel Services

Dear Doctor,

You asked me to carry out a brief strategic procurement review of your operations. I must admit it has been one of the more challenging tasks of my consulting career, but I have made a few high-level recommendations, given below.

1. Your strategy to use 'spot buying' rather than long-term contracts

(other than in a few specialist areas – see point 5) seems very appropriate. Skipping through time of course makes it difficult to commit to volume in any particular time frame that would be relevant for a supplier.

2. Whilst spot buying is probably the only feasible overall strategy, a little more forward planning would help. For instance, planning your re-generation to avoid the usual panic so new items of clothing can be purchased with more notice would help achieve better value for money.

3. There have been some issues with currency – and conventional risk-mitigation strategies such as hedging are also difficult. Will the euro or indeed the $ exist in 200 years' time? We recommend that you convert 50% of your reserves into gold – the one medium of exchange that is ubiquitous on 96% of the known worlds of our galaxy at least.

4. We have been very impressed by your negotiation capability. There is little we can add here to a man who has saved the universe from multiple assailants purely through the power of your logic, rhetoric, charm – even when your apparent BATNA is very weak. Indeed, we believe there is an opportunity for a Who Enterprises negotiation training course, book, online learning programme … The possibilities are endless.

5. However, we observe that spend governance is somewhat weak. It is not at all clear what delegated levels of authority your various companions have held. Some make very major commitments on your behalf whilst others basically run around screaming a lot. We recommend drafting a formal policy and communicating it (telepathically) to your companions.

6. We have, in all truth, failed to observe you personally buying

anything. Ever. We therefore assume that procurement processes are highly automated, with use of infinitely large supplier networks, and little manual intervention needed within the source to pay process. If you were prepared to disclose the solution provider of your platform, you would be a very valuable reference site for that firm, with the potential to monetise that relationship.

7. In certain categories, your procurement appears to be first class. The TARDIS seems to get very regular IT upgrades without any evidence of major installation work. We conclude that the cloud-based platform it runs on, and the perpetual – indeed eternal – licences you purchased some 1,000 years ago represent very good value for money.

8. Whilst it is somewhat outside our remit, the source of your income is also somewhat mysterious. However, we do note today (24/11/2013, earth time) the presence of a holding company – Who Enterprises – on the share registers of Google, Apple and Twitter. And the same firm appears to have sold out of Carillion and Enron shares at just the right moment. We assume this is one of the many benefits of time travel.

I look forward to my presentation to you, and I would be very happy if any of your recent assistants would like to accompany you. Choose your preferred century and galaxy for our meeting, and let me know as soon as possible, so I can hire my time machine at advantageous advance rates.

Yours etc,

***

With apologies to Jonathan Lynn and Peter Jay, I had fun writing the occasional Yes Minister / Prime Minister *spoof. Although I had my suspicions that maybe they weren't always far away from actual discussions in the centre of government…*

Civil Service Performance – Sir Humphrey Speaks

'Ah, Humphrey, do come in.'

'Good morning, Minister, Bernard.'

'So, Humphrey, what do you think of Francis Maude's new idea? Marking all you civil servants and sacking the lowest-ranked performers. What do you think of that, then? Get you and your mandarin friends down the Reform Club in a bit of a lather, I bet?'

'Not at all, Minister, we think it is a wonderful idea. Executed properly, it could improve the support that the civil service can offer you and your colleagues, Minister, which is all we in the upper echelons of the civil service desire!'

'Really? Are you sure, Humphrey? Your colleagues at slightly less exalted levels are a little less happy about the idea.'

'Of course, I understand their concerns. But of course, we will have to do it this properly, that is the key. So, for instance, if Bernard in your office is ranked the lowest of the 20 SCS1 grade managers in this Department, but he is actually performing quite adequately, AND better than perhaps the 5th-ranked SCS1 in another less successful department – the Home Office perhaps – then clearly it wouldn't be fair to dismiss Bernard, now, would it, Minister? That would offend the laws of natural justice, as well as the laws of the land.'

'Well, no, I don't suppose that would be fair in that case …'

'So, we will need to have a standardised review and appraisal process for all Departments with common measures, followed by a cross-organisational moderation process to assess relative performance at each grade, across the whole of Whitehall to ensure fairness and transparency – you do like transparency don't you, Minister?'

'Well, yes …'

'Then of course we will need to go through the proper process. If someone is going to be dismissed for poor performance then we must treat them properly to avoid negative media coverage – so an informal verbal warning, a verbal warning, a first written warning, a second written warning, a final warning, a very final warning… then assuming of course that the informal verbal warning, the verbal warning, the first written warning, the second written warning, the final warning, the very final warning, have all been structured and documented properly, with full evidential support and objective analysis of key performance indicators - then we can fire the sorry specimen!'

'That all sounds a little complicated.'

'Well, you would not want to end up with an embarrassing employment tribunal, Minister, would you?'

'That would be very bad.'

'Then of course we will have to ensure that dismissals are not tainted by – God forbid – racial discrimination, religious preference, the gender and sexual orientation of the employee, age-related issues, disability discrimination of any type …'

'Well, of course not, Humphrey, we wouldn't dream of doing that!'

'So, we will need, I would estimate, several hundred more HR managers across Whitehall to implement this – or consultants if you prefer – plus an extensive training programme, attended by every individual in the civil service who manages staff. We'll have to spend a substantial sum on that training – I've asked our finance Director to set aside £10 million for next year – but I'm sure it will all pay off.'

'Well …'

'Minister, I'm glad you agree. I've already taken the liberty of speaking to the Minister for the Cabinet Office and he has agreed to form a working party of Permanent Secretaries to address these issues. I'm honoured that he has asked me – with your permission of course, Minister – to chair the group. We will agree the terms of reference with the Cabinet then report back in October.'

'Well, at least that's a rapid timetable.'

'October *next year*, Minister. Then a two-year implementation programme I suspect to establish the training, the new appraisal systems, the moderation process …'

'But that will take us well past the next election, Humphrey!'

'Yes Minister. It certainly will.'

***

Government Spend with Smaller Firms – Aspiration or Target?

'Ah Bernard, do come in. We seem to have a bit of a problem. Some of the Government Departments are telling me there's no way they're ever going to hit this target of giving 25% of their procurement spend to small firms – SMEs, I think we call them.'

'Yes Minister. Small and Medium Enterprises. Well, we've already started backtracking – we've made it an *aspiration* rather than a target. And we've said we'll average it across all Departments, AND that it will apply over the full term of the government, not on an annual basis.'

'Does that solve the problem?'

'No Minister. That still doesn't give us enough wiggle room. We have some departments such as DWP and Defence who are never going to get near it, and because they are so large, even averaging it across Whitehall won't help, I fear.'

'Does anyone even care, Bernard? Should I be worried?'

'It does help of course that you are a Conservative-led administration – the Federation of Small Businesses and Chambers of Commerce are always much less forthcoming with their gripes when you are in power, Minister, compared to… when the others are in charge. But eventually even the FSB might catch on. Then we have the usual annoying bloggers who take an interest in these matters …'

'So, what do you suggest we do? Change the target?'

'No Minister. Sir Humphrey and I were talking about this and we had what – forgive me, Minister – we think is rather a good idea.'

'Well, go on, then, man, don't just stand there grinning inanely!'

'Well, we believe it would be quite easy to subtly change the words to include spend with SMEs *in the supply chain* within the 'aspiration' of 25%. Let me explain. So, if you put a contract in place with – let's say – Rolls-Royce, then of course they spend some of their revenue with small firms in their supply chain.'

'Right.'

'Now, we've done the maths …'

'I thought you were all PPE chaps in the senior civil service?'

'Well, we did have to borrow a tame mathematician from the Office for National Statistics … but this is how it works. Let's take MOD. Suppose only 10% of their procurement spend goes to SMEs. The other 90% goes to large firms like Rolls-Royce. Then let's assume that half of that 90% pays for those firms' own staff. The other half – 45% – goes to their suppliers. Now let's assume that 20% of that spend goes to SMEs; so that's another 9% of the MOD's spend gone to the SMEs who are suppliers to the first tier. But of course the sequence continues. Some of the money Rolls-Royce spends with big suppliers also goes to SMEs at the next level down. Now, that gives us an infinite geometric series, which we can sum using the formula a/(1-r) where a is the first term in the series and r is the geometric multiplier.'

'Bernard, my head is beginning to hurt.'

'Almost finished, Minister. In this particular case, if 90% of MOD's spend goes to large companies, and then 20% of each of those suppliers' spend goes to SMEs, and so on ad infinitum. You do know what 'ad infinitum' means, Minister?'

'Yes, yes, go on!'

'Then doing the maths, it means that using our formula, exactly 15% of the MOD's spend goes to SMEs through the supply chain. So, we add that to the 10% that goes directly from MOD and hey presto – we have 25%!'

'Brilliant, Bernard! So do we have a proposal for this subtle change of words?'

'We think something around 'doing business' rather than 'awarding contracts' should do it, Minister. Gives us scope to say that includes the sum to infinity expenditure through the supply chain … What about: *Government's overall aspiration is to do 25% of its business with Small and Medium-sized Enterprises (SMEs)?*

'Bernard, Bernard. You've saved the day again. What would I do without you!? Would you like a small sherry?'

'Thank you. Yes Minister, I rather think I would.'

***

Finally, for this chapter, two not-so-funny but quite personal articles. Back to golf for the first – I'm not a big gambler but the mathematics behind some aspects of it do fascinate me.

Bubba Watson's Win at the Masters Costs Me A Fortune

You may have seen my blog about Bubba Watson and the Masters at the weekend. In it, I made the comment that I had lost £400 because of the amazing recovery shot that effectively won him the tournament and denied Louis Oosthuizen victory – I had money on him.

One of our readers, Rajat Mitra, picked me up on that and said this:

'I'm assuming (and if I'm wrong I wholeheartedly apologise) the £400 would have been your potential 'winnings', not what you actually lost. Probably more 'opportunity cost' loss versus actual 'savings' loss. More of a case of reporting cost avoidance than savings that we in procurement need to be so careful about ...'

Rajat, you are exactly right. It was more of an opportunity cost or potential gain (and we'll probably return to the savings measurement issue as well shortly).

But Betfair, which I use for my occasional forays into gambling, enables you to do some interesting things that actually illustrate key principles of commodity hedging, something that many procurement people do get involved with.

Betfair lets you both place bets for something to happen – as you would with a conventional bookmaker. So, you bet on a horse, or (like me) you bet on Oosthuizen to win the Masters. But with Betfair, you can bet *against* other individual users of the site, who 'offer' the odds to you. When I put £15 on Oosthuizen, on Saturday afternoon, I took the best odds that some other individual was offering on the website – which were 20 to 1.

I then put a further £10 on at 18 to 1 a few minutes later. So, if Oosthuizen – and I – had won, my winnings of around £480 would have come from those unfortunate individuals who bet against him.

Now here comes the clever bit. As the tournament progressed, Oosthuizen started doing better. But I was feeling a bit nervous about losing £25 (last of the big spenders that I am).

So, 24 hours later, I actually put up some of my money to bet *against* him winning. But his odds were now down to around 8 to 1, so I could risk £10 of my money, and if he won, I would have to pay out £80. But of course, if he won, I was going to get 20 times my stake back through my previous bet.

So basically, I reduced my winnings (if he won) from £480 to £400. But were he to lose, my potential losses were now reduced from £25 to £15.

Indeed, if I'd put up £25 of my money against him, I would have reduced my potential winnings to £280 (£480 – £200), but I would have been in a break-even situation if he lost. Clearly, that's what I should have done!

Obviously, this only works if the market moves in your favour, but it is a good example of how firms use hedging strategies, that – IF they do work out – can mean you're in a no-lose situation. Of course, if commodity movements go against you, the opposite can happen. But I'm aware of strategies in areas like currencies that aim to minimise risk while maintaining some upside potential if things do go your way.

However, let's finish with a health warning. Unless you put a lot of effort into it, don't think that you can forecast commodity market movements better than the market!

***

This article stepped well beyond my usual remit, but it is an idea I'd been thinking about for a while, so publishing it seemed like the best way to get it into the public domain and stake my claim to a new concept, or at least a new word to describe the concept! It's not really funny, either.

Wealthopolis

I live 30 miles from London and spend a lot of time in what is arguably the greatest city in the world, now or at anytime in the past (as I've claimed previously). But walking around London, as I often do, not liking taxis or the Tube much, you can get quite disorientated.

Look in an estate agent's window on Sloane Street and see a small mews house – something that would have once housed the family's horses and servants 200 years ago – for sale at £4,500,000. See an ugly jacket or dress in a shop window in the same part of town and if there is a discreet price label, it is likely to be in four if not five figures. Take a look at the menu, or, even better, the wine list, in a Michelin-starred restaurant in London, or indeed in Paris, Tokyo or New York.

I'm lucky; I have earned a decent salary for many years in the UK, still one of the richest countries in the world. Yet these houses, clothes, even bottles of wine, are just way, way out of my league. And it's not just the big capital cities. You will come across this breathtaking wealth in the most desirable beach or skiing resorts the world over – Zermatt in the Alps being a great example, where the smallest apartment will cost you two million euros, and a glass of beer 20 euros in many bars.

It is as if there is another world living in parallel to the one that most of us inhabit. It's a world where paying millions for another property is a casual transaction for its inhabitants, even if it stands empty for most or the entire year. Where buying that bottle of Château Latour to go with your dinner isn't a big deal.

And the inhabitants do interact with us normal folk, but only in strictly controlled and limited ways. They may be in London, but you certainly won't see them on the number 507 bus from Waterloo to Victoria, or in the local Wetherspoons or Starbucks. Their world is with us and around us, but not of us, and not quite connected with our mundane existence. I call this parallel universe *Wealthopolis*.

Wealthopolis is in many locations, if you look carefully, and (sometimes) nowhere, as it exists in hyperspace as well.

It is owned and inhabited by the people who control 99% of the world's wealth. Some of it is clearly distinct – large parts of London, New York or Venice, for instance. Sometimes it is more discreet – a very affluent enclave within an otherwise unremarkable city. Cambridge, for instance, where house prices range from something typical for any pleasant, small British city to astronomical in the space of a mile or so, clearly has a Wealthopolis sector.

Imagine Wealthopolis as an invisible, fifth-dimension cloak lying over certain places, buildings, people, or things. That's how I look at it now anyway. You don't always know immediately when you enter it, but it is there. And some elements of it are open to mere mortals. Many of us can afford the occasional meal in a top restaurant, but other aspects of Wealthopolis are hidden or simply inaccessible. We'll never get an invite to a Bilderberg event, the most exclusive dinners at Davos, Cannes or Glyndebourne, let alone Bill Gates's or Roman Abramovich's private parties.

What is obvious is how Wealthopolis has grown and become clearer in the last few years. The wealth at the top of the tree has increased and asset prices boomed again as governments flood their economies with newly printed money. Central London property prices have grown by 30% since 2008 (and even more in the core Wealthopolis areas) whilst house prices in Birmingham – England's 'second city' – are still around 10% below that 2008 peak. The gap is increasing.

But does this all matter? I think it does. There are practical issues of people being priced out of living in the key Wealthopolis cities. And there is the growing inequality and domination of many aspects of life by the citizens of this new state.

I'm far from being an idealist or a socialist, but how far can inequality go before something cracks? If the richest 1% own 99% of the planet's wealth, is that OK? If they own 99.9%? How about 99.999%? At what point does something snap?

Anyway, if you've got this far, no, there's no great procurement pay-off line here. It's just a thought I wanted to get out there. And you never know, if the term 'Wealthopolis' does take off, remember you read about it here first.

***

Chapter 8

RANDOM OBSERVATIONS

This collection is really just all the articles that didn't quite fall into any of the other categories. The first one here was written on December 28th, as you'll work out.

In Praise of Fairness

This was the first time in 22 years (since her birth) that we didn't have our daughter with us for Christmas Day – she spent it with her boyfriend's parents. We were fine with that, but at her request we pretended December 27th was the big day as they were visiting us by then. So yesterday was our 'Christmas Day', which means we're still a little disorientated here!

Back to daughter – from a remarkably young age, we noticed she had a highly developed sense of fairness. In fact, this innate fairness in children is an interesting research topic for psychologists. It certainly seemed very powerful in her. That wasn't so much in the usual toddler cry of 'it's not fair' when things didn't go her way. It was more how she behaved when playing with her cuddly polar bear toys, and dividing up 'food', or working out whose turn it was amongst her friends to go on the trampoline. Things being fair just seemed to be very important to her.

Which got me thinking, between mince pies and *Doctor Who*, about the importance of the concept in our business lives, as well as our personal, and how dangerous it is for us to underestimate the power of fairness.

If our procurement processes don't give potential suppliers a fair crack of the whip when we're running bidding or sourcing processes, we will store up bad feeling. Or they may simply not bother next time if they don't believe we are being fair. If a supplier 'wins' an electronic auction, but then we just decide to carry on with the incumbent, perhaps having driven their price down a little, is that fair?

How we treat existing suppliers is another example. Suddenly extending payment terms might be within our power if we are a large buyer, but it's probably not fair. Changing agreed contractual terms will be perceived by suppliers as unfair. I rather like the idea of Karma. Eventually, organisations that treat their suppliers badly will get it paid back to them.

Outside procurement, it clearly matters in staff management. I once took over as CPO in an organisation that had unmanageably high staff turnover – it was running at over 30% a year. And one of the main reasons was a perception that key people decisions weren't being made on a fair basis. No one understood why certain people had been promoted, as the process wasn't transparent. The annual bonuses seemed to be allocated on an arbitrary basis, with rumours of favouritism. Someone at a particular management grade had been given a better company car than everyone else at that level.

The effect was corrosive and really negative. Demotivated staff, bad feeling between teams and people, and a high rate of good people exiting. I don't in all honesty claim great success in that or most of my past management roles, but putting in place some clear processes, rules and principles to ensure (as far as possible) fairness was certainly one of my management successes.

At a wider level, effective public administration relies on fairness. We might moan about bureaucratic public procurement processes, or formal recruitment and promotion exercises for public sector jobs, but we mess with that concept of fairness at our peril. Not only does disregarding it create bad feeling, it also leads to poor decisions (the wrong supplier, the less good person for the job). And ultimately, suppliers (or individuals) will invest in non-value adding techniques to win business, looking for personal contacts, bribery or other ways to win if they perceive decisions are made unfairly or arbitrarily.

So, as we approach a New Year, let's celebrate fairness, build on the innate sense that most of us have from the very start of our lives, and remember its power – and the dangers if we lose sight of it.

***

I always have my eyes and ears open for anything that might make a topic for an article. Even an overheard conversation on the train into London.

Managing the Cleaner

On the train into London, early evening, overheard from the seat behind.

'Look, I've never had a cleaner before. And it isn't working out with A… I don't want her to clean my oven. My oven is clean enough already! She took everything out of the bathroom cabinet and cleaned the shelves! I just want the basics done.'

(I couldn't hear the person at the other end, I'm afraid.)

'I'm not criticising her cleaning ability! But I want the lounge hoovered, dusting, the sinks cleaned. I don't want her getting into the detailed areas. I work hard, I don't make much money, I just want someone to take the pressure off a bit. But I got home last night and still had to do all the hoovering myself, she'd spend half her time doing the flaming oven!'

'Well, I've tried to tell her, but she works for you, you explain. It doesn't seem to get through. I want the whole house cleaned, but only the important stuff, and three hours should be enough for that – it's only a small place.'

This went on for some time – my heart went out to the lady, who clearly wasn't being unreasonable, but had failed to get the message through. I wanted to turn around and say, 'Write down and agree a detailed specification, with clear performance indicators and agreed review mechanisms.' However, I got the impression that English probably wasn't the cleaner's first language, and of course the lady may not have been too pleased with my eavesdropping …

But it made me think about outsourcing and potential problems. Here was a real disconnect between customer and provider, and a breakdown of communication. The cleaner probably thinks she's doing a great job. 'Look! Their oven is beautiful'. I also suspect that the cleaning firm was trying to build up the work: 'you need more than three hours a week, we can't do all you need in that time'.

And the client? Well, the client didn't want to buy a high-specification service, or to buy a greater quantity of output. She was very happy with the basic-level service, done to a reasonable standard of performance.

So, what lessons can we draw from this? Well, sometimes it's not the client pushing for 'higher quality', it can be the provider – sometimes with ulterior motives. And there's no shame in just wanting the basic service if that meets your needs.

But whatever you want, you have to find a way of communicating it clearly to the provider, or you can guarantee that distressed phone calls will ensue!

***

Here are a few articles about procurement strategy, role, structure etc. Not always the most exciting topics, but very important, nonetheless.

'Supporting the Business' – Not Enough for Procurement

We commented recently on the confusion, evident at the ProcureCon Indirect conference in London, around the role of procurement. That is probably more striking when we look at 'Indirect' procurement, given the more obvious role and legitimacy of procurement in the direct space. (It's unusual to find a plant manager insisting on buying their own automotive components in that industry, for instance, in the way we may well see the marketing director wanting to retain control over media buying.)

Back to the conference. Some presenters still talked about global leverage and organisation-wide strategic sourcing and category management programmes. These organisations are pursuing an approach that indicates procurement has some overarching governance role in terms of managing spend or suppliers across the organisation. That category imperative can take precedence over the wishes of an individual line manager, if there is a demonstrable benefit to the wider organisation.

But other presenters came from major organisations that have abandoned wider category management programmes. They talked about the role of procurement as supporting the front-line business. Or, to be more precise (because this is what such a role means in practice), supporting key individual budget-holding senior executives in business or other functional areas. So that might be the General Manager of a business division, or the CIO or Marketing VP.

Now that's fine, up to a point. Clearly, procurement must always be cognisant of the needs and desires of budget holders. Indeed, in some organisations, that supporting role may be the only one that procurement is ever likely to take. If the organisation is resolutely devolved and decentralised, perhaps also with a highly entrepreneurial bent, then it may act in practice more like a loose affiliation of independent organisations than a single corporate entity. In such cases, probably the only feasible strategy for procurement is to focus on supporting local management in whatever way they want.

But for most organisations, we would argue this narrow focus means procurement is not adding as much value as it might to the overall organisation. In *Buying Professional Services* (which I co-wrote in 2010 with Fiona Czerniawska), we described three roles for procurement people, and one of them we called the 'Faithful Servant'. This was applied to Professional Services procurement, obviously, but has wider application. Here's a taste of what we said:

> Faithful servants' see their role as enablers, supporting users in their engagement of the professional service firm. The purchasing team may assist, but only where the user wants them to. They may get involved in selecting suppliers and setting out some basic standard terms and conditions, but it is always at the request of the user. If the user decides to manage the procurement and relationship with the supplier themselves, then they will politely withdraw.

So, what's wrong with this approach? It has obvious positives – one might assume that choosing suppliers that really meet the needs of the business is a pretty good idea, surely? And procurement working where it is wanted rather than forcing ourselves on managers has some merits? Yes, but as we went on to say:

> The dangers of this are clear ... the 'faithful servant' approach can end up with chaotic, poorly controlled spend patterns. Lack of governance over the purchasing process, lack of objectivity

in selecting suppliers and negotiating contracts can lead to supplier choice based purely on friendships and personal prejudices. Suppliers find themselves in a position where they can economically exploit the buying organisation. Selling becomes a case of developing strong relationships with key decision-makers, rather than proving you have the best value business solution.

That extract highlights what we might call the governance role of the procurement function. Spend governance means overarching controls and rules about who can spend the organisation's money and (critically from a procurement aspect), how it is to be spent. In our experience, being the guardians of the governance, and playing a role in educating colleagues about it, and indeed policing it, is a key role for procurement. Where procurement works purely at the invitation of management, it is likely that such governance will be weaker.

And there are other business risks in that 'faithful servant' procurement approach. For instance, if multiple budget holders have freedom in their choice of suppliers, the overall supplier and supply situation is not managed. If many managers in different business areas choose the same supplier, for instance, at organisational level you might see an unhealthy supplier dependence emerge or an unacceptable risk profile. Who is managing that bigger picture and, if necessary, making decisions that take into account the whole organisation's perspective?

What about leverage? Economies of scale are often overestimated by procurement and others in our view, but there are undoubted opportunities that can and should be exploited – again, a disaggregated approach with budget holders calling all the shots loses any chance of that.

So, as you can tell, I'm not a great fan of the 'faithful servant' model. That doesn't mean, to emphasise again, that procurement can afford to be neglectful of understanding and responding to the needs of their budget-holding stakeholders. But it does mean positioning the role as something more than simply doing whatever that stakeholder wants procurement to do for them – or indeed accepting a situation where the stakeholder just wants procurement out of their hair completely!

***

Inventing the SCAN (see below) is one of my lasting contributions to the procurement world. OK, its not exactly the Kraljic Matrix but hey, I'm doing my best!

CLAN and SCAN

Our first newsletter drew some comments and the one I valued and enjoyed most was from Dr Richard (Dick) Russill. Dick is a hero and mentor of mine and has probably done as much as anyone alive in the UK to develop, promote and educate in the procurement field over the last 40 years as a trainer, writer, adviser, educator…

Anyway, Dick said the newsletter was: 'a surreal mix of hardcore procurement and cerebral whimsy', which I thought was a great description!

But, on more serious matters, way back in the mists of time, Dick invented and proposed the concept of CLAN as a procurement strategy and organisational structure for large organisations – *the Centre-Led Action Network*. The basic premise (skip a paragraph if you know this) was an organisational design and operating approach for procurement based on a small procurement centre, probably including the CPO, setting strategy and gathering information from the centre of the organisation.

But the main procurement operations were to be carried out in a devolved fashion around the network of business units. Procurement staff would report locally, but with a dotted line to a CPO or equivalent in the centre. Lead category management responsibility would be allocated out around the procurement staff in the network, but with some guidance and loose control from the centre.

A few years ago, I decided to go for a new acronym and invented the SCAN – the Strategically Controlled Action Network. My argument was that CLAN suffered from being a bit woolly in practice; procurement people tended to take the local priorities as their main driver and the small team in the centre was often left with little real authority to drive collaboration or improvement.

So SCAN looked at a structure with geographically devolved networks of procurement professionals – but with those people having line reporting to the centre and the CPO. More direct control could then be exerted over key activities. I stick by that view, although I have to say SCAN (certainly as a bit of procurement jargon) never caught on in the way that CLAN did.

But I've been thinking recently about how these and other potential organisational structures have been impacted by the development of procurement technology. Has the huge growth in capability of sourcing, P2P, spend analytics and other technology changed the view of the optimal organisational structure for a leading-edge procurement function in a large organisation? (Or even perhaps across organisations, as for instance in the case of the UK Government's collaboration initiative.)

The concept of CLAN is a small management centre, keeping strategic control of the procurement function without having direct line management. The question is whether you need to exert line management authority in order to ensure your organisational procurement strategy is implemented properly? Do you need to have the power of the annual appraisal and pay award in order to get procurement people working as you want them to as CPO of a large organisation?

I had my doubts – hence the SCAN concept I invented which gave the centre more real power. But actually, I now believe that technology makes it more feasible to 'control' procurement across a devolved, dispersed organisation than ever before; even without the added power that comes from having direct line reporting of procurement staff. So, I would suggest that, as the CPO, I could quite easily exert strategic control without worrying about reporting lines, particularly if I have all or most of the following:

- Regular data available via strong spend analytics processes so I know what is being spent, where, by whom, with which suppliers.
- A single view of vendor master data, fed by common supplier information processes for all my major suppliers globally.
- Spend data to support aggregation and leverage, use collaborative tools (panel scoring of bids etc.) across the dispersed team and run major sourcing events (where appropriate) with multiple internal participants.
- An organisation-wide sourcing process, supported by technology that provides an audit trail of how the process has been followed.
- A 'no PO, no payment' philosophy across the organisation, so I can see every requisition and purchase order being placed across the organisation and have sign-off on the largest.
- Regular automated reports of orders and spend against our database of existing contracts and approved suppliers.
- An organisation-wide contract / supplier management process,

including SRM (supplier relationship management) for my
critical suppliers, with standardised repotting of KPIs and
similar.
• A performance management process that measures real savings
  and the drivers of savings / cost changes by category…

Now this is an exaggerated and idealised picture of course; but
all these elements are very possible now. They weren't going back
10 years or so – or at least not without huge cost and difficulty.
However, there is a paradox here. We're suggesting that 'control'
can be exerted through common use of processes and technology,
without direct reporting lines. But of course, getting that use of
common systems and processes is not easy without having the direct
control to ensure everyone implements them! So, we shouldn't
underestimate the difficulty of getting to this point.

But having said that, there seems little doubt that a CPO sitting
in London, Chicago, JoBurg or Munich can direct and manage a
dispersed function – whatever the reporting lines – better than ever
before through appropriate use of technology. (And even at a local
level, the same applies to a head of function in any sized organisation
who is perhaps looking to 'control' internal stakeholders who don't
report directly to procurement.)

So has technology swung the pendulum back towards CLAN
rather than SCAN? Well, despite the fact that Dick Russill invented
CLAN when most of this technology was just a gleam in a teenage
Jason Busch's eye, I think it has.

Ironically, my feeling is that many organisations have been
tightening up direct line control in recent years (towards SCAN
rather than CLAN), perhaps in a response to challenging economic
circumstances and a higher awareness of supply chain risk. But
technology certainly gives organisations the opportunity now to

combine local line management of the procurement team, which has some benefits, with real central control over the key levers of procurement power, strategy and process.

**

Everyone loves using prime contractors, don't they? So nothing like stirring things up a bit and going against the general orthodoxy!

Prime Contractors – Sensible Procurement Tool or a Soft Option

Once upon a time in procurement, when we wanted to buy something – goods or services – we identified someone who could sell that to us. In some cases, a supplier might offer more than one product, or even quite different products, but generally they sold us what they produced.

The exception was 'agents'. Particularly when buying from foreign suppliers, they would act as an intermediary. As well as dealing with the primary producer of the material or product, they might also arrange transport, and handle import and insurance requirements as part of their value-added contribution. Early in my career, buying ingredients and raw materials for the food industry, I would use agents for products ranging from milk powder to colours and flavours.

Then matters started getting more complicated. At some point, a new role started to develop, called different things in different industries and sectors, but perhaps most commonly termed the 'Prime contractor'. I suspect the construction industry was where we first saw this being used in a serious and frequent way.

Rather than engaging different people or firms to carry out

different tasks, why not put an overall project manager in charge? That could be one of the firms who actually carried out some of the direct work, but who could also take on the overall management of the entire project. Or it might be an individual or organisation whose entire task would be the management of the overall project and the suppliers who contributed towards it.

Wouldn't that be easier for the buyer? Only one supplier to deal with, and one party to take on the overall responsibility?

Yes, in many cases, it has proved easier and better for the buyer. Certainly, in construction, that is now the standard approach and few buyers would now look to engage directly with different firms or individuals to do the groundwork, bricklaying, carpentry, electrical installation, and so on. Trying to manage this and allocate responsibility – and blame if anything went wrong – would be time-consuming and challenging.

But more recently again, this model has spread way beyond construction into a whole range of other industries and sectors. It has grown considerably in the IT market, where firms might offer overall management of desktop computing services, for example. The specific 'Systems Integrator' term was created to define this sort of role in bringing together different technology and processes under a Prime contractor.

In facilities management, we've seen the growth of the TFM (total facilities management) concept. A single supplier will provide a whole range of services such as repairs and maintenance, catering, cleaning, security. But almost always that involves some other firms as part of the supply chain, all managed through the TFM provider.

We now see the Prime concept emerging strongly in the contingent / interim staff engagement field, where a managed service provider, usually a single vendor, takes responsibility for all management of interim staff, usually with a network of subcontractors. And in wider Business Process Outsourcing (BPO), we're increasingly seeing firms offering to provide a whole range of services, only some of which they will deliver themselves. In the UK government sector, for instance, one local council has bundled up call centre operations, payroll, IT, Human Resources services, corporate procurement and estate management into a single outsourcing contract.

Now, unlike the original model of Prime contractors, some of those services bear only the faintest of direct relationships to each other. So, if we consider the construction example, there is a clear linkage between the elements that are brought together under the Prime – in particular, they all contribute to the single end product, the building of the house.

But we now see perhaps Finance, Human Resources, and Procurement, bundled together in a Business Process Outsourcing package. Or even in terms of the typical TFM portfolio of activities, there is little real synergy between operating the catering facility in a large office and fixing the roof.

Indeed, in the UK public sector in particular, this model is causing arguments that go well beyond the procurement community – controversy, legal action and public outcry has kept us busy on Spend Matters UK / Europe in terms of coverage of local councils outsourcing activities in Cornwall, Barnet and Somerset, for instance.

Somewhere in all of this, have we lost sight of why Prime Contracting first seemed like a good idea? We can probably all agree that in the construction example, there are major benefits in having one party taking on the overall responsibility for delivering a single finished product to the customer. That's not to say this approach is free of disadvantages, even in this case, but it isn't difficult to argue that the benefits outweigh the negatives.

But when we bundle up activities that aren't so clearly related, and hand them over to a single Prime contractor, are the pros and cons really being considered properly? Is this happening for the right business reasons, or purely because it is fashionable and looks like it should make life easier?

***

Prime Contractors – Pros and Cons to Consider

Let's take a rational and structured look at the pros and cons of using prime contractors.

Positives

Primes were originally used in areas such as construction for good reasons – they undoubtedly made life better and easier for the buyer. Here's why.

Convenience – the buying organisation can (in the main) deal with just one organisation – the prime contractor. This simplifies the task and makes managing the contract and the business around it simpler.

Cost of contract management – that simplification also has an impact on the cost of contract and supplier management. At its most basic, managing just one supplier reduces the cost of contract management compared to managing multiple parties.

Clarity on risk ownership – or as we might paraphrase, there's only one supplier to kick! The prime should be carrying the greater part of the overall supply chain risk, so if there are issues, the buyer has a clear point of contact and responsibility. In theory, at least.

Standardisation – in some areas, a single prime can help to drive standardisation of goods or services. Whilst this may still require serious effort, it may be easier for the prime to take the lead on that (rather than the ultimate buyer) given their position in, or knowledge of, the market.

Compliance – it can sometimes be easier to drive compliance through a contractual route with a prime contractor, rather than persuade internal stakeholders to follow a multiple supplier preferred list, for instance. This has worked well in some UK public sector organisations – driving better compliance in the temporary staff market through a VMS-type prime has been generally successful.

Economies of scale – in some cases, bundling work together can drive economies of scale that the buyer, if they're smart, can capture. But it is a myth that putting additional volume into a contract will always achieve economies of scale – consider a prime managing a range of very different second-tier providers. There is minimal volume benefit for the prime and no real economies that can be passed on to the buyer.

Negatives
However, there are negatives as well around use of Primes. They will apply differently in different situations, but here are some points that should always be considered.

Cost – in most cases, the Prime is going to add on a margin to cover their costs of managing the supply chain and (probably) accepting more overall risk. At the very least, the buyer should ensure they have visibility of these costs.

Loss of visibility of the supply chain – if the prime is controlling other players in the supply chain, whether at different tiers or in a network manner, the buyer may find it difficult to understand or have visibility of the wider supply base. That can lead to issues ranging from reputational risks that may not even be perceived by the buyer, to a lack of value for money via the supply chain.

Innovation – in most cases, a supplier 'down' the supply chain is less likely to share real innovation with the buyer if there is a prime in the way. Suppliers share innovation when they feel valued and there is trust between the parties – which seems less likely when the relationship is not even a direct contractual one.

Resilience – again, the lack of a direct relationship can bring issues if, for instance, there are shortages or supply chain interruptions in the market. As in the case of innovation, firms are more likely to give supply priority to those buyers with whom they have a direct relationship. Using a prime can also mean that information about issues takes longer to reach the ultimate buyer; which can be a problem in a crisis situation.

Risk allocation – whilst there may be good reasons for allowing the prime to take risk, it is not necessarily the best way of allocating risk through the supply chain. Risk is usually best allocated to whichever party can best manage it, and that may not be the prime. There is also the danger that the buyer does not have full visibility or understanding of the risk profile – until something goes wrong!

Management – managing a prime who is playing an important role in coordinating a complex supply chain requires very effective contract management. There's an irony that often firms go the prime route because they feel it will minimise their required contract management effort – forgetting that managing the prime is vitally important and can be just as challenging as managing a range of less critical providers.

Conclusions

It should be clear from this checklist and brief discussion that using a prime, particularly for anything important, high-risk or significant, is not a decision to be taken lightly. It requires careful thought, and we would recommend a business case that considers the 'for' and 'against' arguments in a structured and unbiased manner.

There are times when a Prime contractor is the best option – few would want to manage a major construction project without any sort of a Prime arrangement. But too many organisations have been using the technique because of what they perceive to be convenience, without fully considering the negatives. So, do think carefully about both sides of the argument before making a decision.

***

Here's a topic that procurement still hasn't addressed properly, I'd argue.

Clearing Out My Study – Contract Management Fail

Clearing out my study the other day was a somewhat depressing experience. Not just because of the huge quantities of papers I've collected over the years, and my wavering around whether to ditch many years' worth of Supply Management magazines – will I ever need them again? Will they become valuable collector's items one day? I still bitterly regret throwing out in the early 90s several hundred copies of the New Musical Express from the late 70s through the 80s, then discovering a few years later they were worth at least a fiver a copy …

But the real downer was realising how true 'plus ça change, plus c'est la même chose' is when it comes to procurement. Are things really progressing? Are we more skilled and effective as a profession than we were 10 years ago?

As I went through this material, this really hit me. Here's a really leading-edge presentation from a conference, painting a vision of e-procurement, supplier networks and collaboration that looks bang up to date. But the footer gives the game away – this is from May 2001. The vision hasn't moved on much at all since then, and 95% of organisations are still miles away from turning it into reality.

Then I came across a box full of material all around contract and supplier management. A strategic supplier programme I helped to introduce to the Department of Education in 2002. A review with a financial services firm shortly after that. Some supporting papers for various projects I did with OGC and the Treasury over the years in central Government. Reports from other experts like Future Purchasing, guidance published by various organisations that I got my hands on to inform the work I was doing. Then a major piece of work I did with the National Audit Office in 2007 – which led to some output I'm still proud of today.

But if you asked 100 CPOs today – is your organisation better at contract and supplier management then it was 10 years ago – I wonder how many could truly say 'yes'? And in how many of them would we see the procurement function having a clearly defined role in the contract and supplier management process, across all the key third party contracts in the business?

Indeed, there's still a procurement school of thought that says, 'contract management is nothing to do with us'. Some of that comes from the fact that procurement can't possibly take the lead on managing every major contract in their organisation – inevitably other functions or business lines will own some key contracts. So, some procurement people think that if they can't lead it all, it's better to let others just get on with it.

Even our Institute has been uncertain how to approach it. CIPS (the Chartered Institute of Procurement and Supply) hasn't been comfortable with other functions (and non-qualified people) 'doing procurement'. I think that's been a point of conflict. The view may be that if we bring contract managers into the CIPS professional family, next thing you know there'll be lots of non-professionals wanting to let contracts themselves.

However, there are very strong arguments for procurement taking a lead here in terms of owning the overall responsibility for contract and supplier management in their organisations. That doesn't mean doing everything themselves; but it does mean taking a lead in certain key areas. Why?

Firstly, contract management is simply very important – in pretty much every organisation. With our interconnected, outsourced, collaborative world, getting what we've contracted for out of our most critical suppliers, and managing them in a positive manner, is usually an essential success factor for the client organisation.

And if procurement doesn't take overall ownership of this, who will? Who will own the overarching governance of contract and supplier management, who will look at capability, processes, and systems on an organisational wide basis?

But ultimately, the most important reasons for procurement leadership and involvement (and I'm not arguing we can DO everything ourselves, remember) is simple. We can't say that we've been successful in procurement until the contract has been actually *delivered* – not just signed. Success must mean that the goods or services were appropriate, that the supplier performance, price, quality, and service were as we contracted for in the first place. So, we'd argue that it would be rash and risky for procurement to leave this key determinant of procurement success purely in the hands of others.

Consider this – and I don't think many experienced procurement people would disagree with this analysis. Of course, it's simplified and generic, but it is broadly true.

Good contract + good contract management = Successful outcome
Good contract + lousy contract management = Unsuccessful outcome
Bad contract + good contract management = (Possibly) successful outcome
Bad contract + lousy contract management = Unsuccessful outcome

What this says is that bad contract management can mess up *even the best contract*, and good contract management can often recover an initially poor contract or supplier. So arguably, the strength of the contract management is more important even than the initial procurement.

Basically, we're arguing that good contract management is an absolutely necessary condition for a successful outcome from that contract and therefore a successful outcome to the procurement process.

So, that should convince everyone that it is in procurement's own interest to take contract management seriously. But as we said, procurement can't manage every contract fully and unilaterally in a hands-off manner. We have to find ways of agreeing who does what, with the business or other functions who have a legitimate interest in supplier and contract performance. That's still an absolutely key issue here.

***

It isn't always serious pontification on the future of procurement, though. Sometimes, I could combine work and pleasure.

Windsor & Eton

Purely, you understand, in the interests of supply chain and blogging research, and at great personal sacrifice, I signed up for a trip recently to a brewery. I know, it's a tough job but someone has to do it …

So, on a typical English summer evening (torrential rain and moderately chilly) around 15 of us, all ex-Mars Group employees, gathered in a Windsor backstreet under the shadow of the Castle to meet three ex-Mars managers and a fourth colleague who have realised the dream of many executives of a certain age by starting their own brewery.

Two of them I know from my days at Mars Confectionery, although I hadn't seen either for many years until recently. Indeed, Jim Morrison, the process engineer of the team, started at Mars on the graduate trainee scheme the same day as me.

They founded the Windsor & Eton Brewery (WEB) in 2010, 79 years after the closure of Windsor's last brewery, and they are brewing some truly excellent beers in the royal town. We will get onto some interesting procurement and supply chain points that emerged from the evening, but let me say a bit about the business and the beers first. You can jump a few paragraphs if you don't like beer …

The brewery has been very successful, with revenues approaching the £1 million mark this year. The founders aren't trying to be the next InBev; but neither are they playing at this as a hobby. Apart from anything, just spending a couple of hours on the premises illustrates what a tough job it is as a micro-brewer!

Most importantly perhaps, the product is excellent. We won't go through the whole range of beers but their most widely sold draught bitters are Guardsman, Windsor Knot and the golden ale Knight of the Garter. They're all very good indeed and thoroughly recommended if you're lucky enough to live near a pub serving them (there's a list on their website).

And special mentions for Conqueror, an unusual and delicious Black IPA. It looks and pours like a Guinness-type stout, but has a flavour that is closer to a bitter IPA than the sweetness of a stout. But my personal favourite from the tasting was the Kohinoor IPA, named after the diamond in The Queen's crown, and the second new brew they've introduced in this Jubilee year of 2012. Not surprisingly they're playing on the royal links with Windsor, so they've brewed a TreeTops with African flavours, and now the Kohinoor with an Indian theme.

What has been the main driver behind the incredible growth in small breweries in the UK? (We now have over 800, more than pretty much anywhere else in the world.) And what do you think the most critical element or component of the supply chain is for a small 'craft brewer' – and increasingly for the big boys as well?

The answer to both these questions is 'hops'.

You may know that hops, along with malted barley, yeast and water are the basic ingredients of beer. But I had no idea of the revolution in hop production that has taken place over the last 20 years or so. Will Calvert of WEB started his career at Courage's Brewery some 30 years ago and he explained that the entire huge Courage operation at that time used just three or four varieties of hops. WEB, a tiny fraction of that scale, uses 15 varieties already for their range, and Wikipedia lists 110 separate hop varieties!

Hops were seen until recently as simply adding the bitterness element to the brew early in the process. But a boom in breeding and developing new varieties, with different flavours and aromas, has allowed brewers to produce an ever-expanding range of ales, appealing to different tastes. Hops are also now added to the mix at different stages of the brewing process, to give further sensory options, so you will see beers that are 'twice-hopped', for instance. In the case of beers such as WEB's Treetops and Kohinoor, other flavour ingredients are also increasingly included.

This has truly turned the beer market into something seen as fashionable, innovative and worthy of the serious expert attention that the wine industry has enjoyed for years. Pontificating over aromas, the nose, the length of the finish and so on is no longer purely the preserve of the wine connoisseur!

But it has thrown up some new supply chain issues. The most valued and prized hops can cost at least five times more than the standard or traditional varieties such as the English Fuggles. The market has become global, with sought-after hops grown in the USA, Eastern Europe and Australia / New Zealand. That brings issues of supply chain management and risk – transport, currency fluctuations, natural disasters, and so on.

And brewers (or their purchasing managers) have to look at options around forward commitment to guarantee supply of scarce varieties. Will Calvert had bought some physical stocks of some varieties months ahead to obtain what he needs in terms of key ingredients for his beers – but that of course can bring issues of cash flow, storage and planning. We haven't quite got to formal futures trading for hops, or counting the young flowers on the plants to predict the crops (as happens in the case of cocoa) but perhaps one day we will!

***

The Proxima report referred to in the next piece was and is very significant for procurement. But my 'decline' article that follows did question whether the success of the procurement profession in recent years will necessarily continue. More controversy!

Proxima Report – Corporate Virtualisation

Last autumn, we featured a fascinating piece of research by procurement outsourcing service providers Proxima. The firm looked at the accounts of 350 FTSE companies to see how much those firms spent on third-party costs versus internal staff costs.

Now Proxima has repeated the exercise but this time on a global basis, with a major emphasis on US firms. Their research is captured in a new report, just published, which seeks to understand the cost base of organisations across the globe, by analysing the cost base of almost 2,000 businesses across 58 countries for 2009, 10 and 11.

In the report, various senior executives talk about the importance of addressing supply costs rather than thinking chopping headcount is the easiest way of saving money. And there's a typically left field (but accurate) quote from Guy Strafford of Proxima:

> The analogy I use is that it's like swimming in the sea. There are times when you can see down 10ft, then suddenly you look down and you can't see the bottom. It's a bit like that in terms of organisations understanding their suppliers: there can be a whole level that's invisible to them.

Anyway, back to the report. The results are just as startling as they were for the UK report. Across the sample of 2,000 firms, internal staff costs accounted for (on average) 12.5% of revenues. By contrast, third party costs represented 69.9%. And that's up from 66% in 2009.

Almost 70%! Far more than the 50% or so I've been quoting in presentations and reports for most of my career. Clearly, this data should be superb ammunition for anyone arguing the importance of procurement activity, and suppliers, to their organisation. That's five times as much expenditure going to third parties as being spent on staff. Yet how much discussion does each topic get at Board level? Who is more senior – the CPO or the HR Director?

But the Proxima report gives more than just the bald figures. It gets into a perceptive discussion around the trends that have led us to this point, because certainly the numbers would have looked very different 50, 30 or even 10 years ago. Why has that 'external' percentage grown so much? And is it likely to reverse anytime soon? ('No' is the unsurprising answer to that latter question.)

And it also looks at what this means to organisations. There's the financial calculation, for a start, that says saving 1% on supplier costs is going to boost profits far more than a similar saving on staff costs. But there's also the obvious boost to procurement's cause, emphasising the need for effective supplier engagement and management. And perhaps more importantly in the greater scheme of things, what are the consequences for CEOs in terms of overall business strategies and approaches? What does it mean (or perhaps, what *should* it mean) to be running a business where close to 70% of your revenues are spent with suppliers?

That all makes it essential material to have in your library – a vital tool to help stakeholder engagement and promotion of the whole procurement raison d'être!

In the report, Proxima proposes three main reasons for this growth in third-party spend – technology, specialisation and globalisation. Technology means that you have to be truly expert to keep up with and exploit the latest developments, which most businesses can't do without help.

Specialisation is a similar driver – no organisation can be good at everything these days, in our complex world, so outsourcing and buying in goods and services rather than internal production is the order of the day. Finally, globalisation, through factors such as currency liberalisation, free trade and better transport options, has made buying easier and the options much wider and more attractive.

The end result, as Proxima put it, is 'what was once a pay slip, is now a supplier invoice'.

I might add to that something around flexibility, both operational and financial. Firms are sensitive to working capital and funding issues, so buying in rather than making internal investment is often favoured. And the flexibility to reduce or increase purchases quickly depending on market conditions is another benefit of sourcing externally.

These underlying reasons behind the growth in third-party spend suggest this trend isn't going to reverse anytime soon. One might assume, however, that there is some point at which it will stop – an organisation with no employee cost might be a step too far! But there seems no reason why that 69.9% external cost figure couldn't reach 80 or even 90% in some firms.

Yet this raises a number of questions. The report draws the conclusion, quite rightly, that getting more out of suppliers should sit right at the heart of the CEO's priority list. Taking 1% out of third-party costs will have far more impact on the bottom line that doing the same for staff costs. But it is not just the financials – the risk and governance elements around supply chains are significant, and the Proxima report highlights these as another reason for strong supply base focus. 'Business leaders should seek greater assurance that activities in their extended and more complex supply chains are acceptable', as it says.

So, the case for investment in this area appears to be very strong. But we also know that procurement and supplier issues in many firms aren't priorities. And, more often than not, the Human Resources Director outranks the Chief Procurement Officer, and supply or supplier-related issues are rarely debated at Board level.

That gap in top-level understanding is emphasised by the interviews undertaken as part of the study, with 44 Board-level executives. They were asked what percentage of their revenue they thought was attributable to supplier costs. Only one executive estimated the number to be greater than 40%. And all 44 'expressed surprise' when they were told just what the real number was.

So senior people are vastly underestimating the scale and therefore presumably the importance of suppliers in their business – indeed, they're often something like 100% out in their estimates, guessing at 30-40% instead of 60-80%!

That's a worrying fact, yet one that clearly shows an opportunity as well, both for organisations generally to increase focus and for procurement leaders to use this to drive better performance. But it is worth considering for a moment why this situation has arisen.

It's not a great reflection on the Board frankly that they don't understand their own cost base. But maybe that is in part down to how firms generally budget and run their financial management processes. Costs are generally looked at on a cost centre basis, with less emphasis on how that money is spent. So, the CFO would (we would hope) have a good grip on spend by cost centre, and perhaps by major project, but has less visibility on where that money goes, and how much to suppliers as opposed to staff.

One question therefore we might ask is whether CFOs need to look at some different reporting mechanisms that might come part of the standard suite of reports and would give them that better visibility of supplier spend?

The other point emerging from this lack of current visibility is the relationship between the CPO (Procurement Director or equivalent), the CFO and the Board. An effective CPO should make sure their top management understand the importance of the supply base, including the scale of the spend. Clearly, in the firms surveyed here, that isn't happening well enough. Either the CPO isn't aware of the scale of the spend either, or they don't communicate it to senior colleagues. That could be because of lack of skills, opportunity or desire.

One other thought around the lack of awareness, and that is the question of what we consider to be third-party spend. At one level, it may include areas that clearly fit into a conventional definition of supplier spend, but have not been within scope for the procurement function – perhaps banking services, or even marketing in some organisations.

Then there is spend that some don't consider as 'procurement' – I had an argument with one organisation recently about financial 'grants' they were making to individuals and businesses for specific purposes. They did not consider this to be anything even vaguely related to procurement; but my argument was that they were choosing entities to perform a certain service on their behalf. Whatever they called it, to me it certainly sounded like 'procurement'!

Then we have some areas such as rent and property taxes, which are definitely third-party spend but with some justification may not be considered under the procurement banner. All of this can lead to some confusion, so a good starting point for CPOs is to define clearly what the organisation considers as third-party spend.

Anyway, what is crystal-clear from the Proxima report is that procurement leaders, CFOs, CEOs and others should understand their cost base, where the money is going, who the most important suppliers are, and other key metrics. And communicating that to the Board should be an absolutely fundamental priority for procurement leaders.

***

Is Procurement in Decline?

We have explained previously why the growth in outsourcing and vertical 'disintegration' of supply chains over the last 40 years has led to a multiplier effect in terms of the procurement workload through the supply chain. That in turn has driven the impressive growth of the procurement profession and associated industries.

So, why might that trend be at a point of inflexion? Has the growth stopped, and might it even start going the other direction? That seems very likely.

Firstly, there must be some sort of limit on the whole process or outsourcing – organisations cannot outsource 100% of their activity, or at least if they do, it's impossible for them to create sustainable added value. (Could Ford totally outsource the manufacture of cars and become simply a marketing organisation? Yes, but one assumes that might not be a good move from a competition standpoint.) So, we might assume that there is some point beyond which organisations generally cannot go in terms of that percentage of revenues that is accounted for by third-party spend.

We might argue that Apple has gone about as far as anyone can in this regard, keeping product design and marketing as their vital in-house competencies and outsourcing manufacturing almost totally. But maybe this illustrates our point – the firms that can do this are already there. It's hard to see how Apple could *increase* that percentage of revenues going to third-party suppliers.

Secondly, the supply chain risk profile has begun to turn in favour of having greater control over the supply chain. I don't see us returning to the Henry Ford vertical integration days, but the risk and control arguments are becoming more thoughtful after some decades where the 'outsource everything' mantra was dominant. So, we are seeing a more generally critical mood afoot in terms of assessing the benefits of outsourcing. They may be no more than straws in the wind, but some high-profile rejections of outsourcing in the UK public sector, and BT's announcement that they are bringing facilities management services back in house, may indicate at the very least a more diligent examination of the business case for outsourcing.

And finally, and perhaps most importantly, the reducing cost advantage associated with offshoring will make many organisations in Europe and the US look again at supply chain and sourcing decisions. And if you're going to buy components or part-finished goods from down the road instead of China, then you may at least consider whether you should produce them yourself rather than buying from a third party.

If our hypothesis is correct, that percentage of revenues going to third-party suppliers won't grow much more and may even start to decline. That will obviously reduce procurement workload. But, I hear you say, there are still many category spend areas that procurement doesn't influence within organisations. Won't that be our major source of growth over the next 10 years, as we continue our push to increase our traction over non-traditional and indirect areas? Well, it might. I'm not claiming absolute certainty here. But there are three reasons why this may not be enough to save us from a decline in 'professional' numbers.

Firstly, given that we see so many examples of bad procurement practice in these areas, it is by no means a given that more and more organisations will entrust their marketing, professional services or FM spend to procurement professionals. Now this at least is somewhat within our own control – the better we can get at this as a profession, the more chance we have of continuing the land grab we've made over the last 20 years.

But I'm also seeing some signs that organisations, whilst

recognising the importance of good procurement activities, don't necessarily see that sitting in a procurement function. Talking to people from a large financial services firm recently, they told me that the IT Procurement people (for instance) were now sitting in the IT function. 'With a dotted line to the central Procurement team?' I asked. No, the central team and Procurement Director were gone.

Under this scenario, procurement activity might grow, but with people executing it who will not necessarily see themselves as core members of 'our' profession.

And finally, while overall outsourcing may have peaked, outsourcing of procurement itself may get more prevalent. If we see more of that, particularly in the indirect spend areas, which I believe we will, there must be some consequent economies of scale. One assumes that the outsourcers will be able to serve multiple clients with fewer professional staff in total than if each client did it themselves. So, whilst there may still be a contract / supplier management role (the intelligent customer) left on the client side, the net effect will be a decline in professional numbers.

Now, as I say, this is all just speculation and hypothesis. But it's good to look critically at where procurement sits. Most of what you read from folk with a vested interest – CIPS, consulting firms or whatever – paints a not altogether unexpected picture of the profession as a roaring success, which arguably it has been for the last 20 years or more. But let's just be aware that past success doesn't necessarily mean things will continue like that forever.

And that in turn should make us keener than ever to get better at what we do.

***

Chapter 9

ADVICE TO
SOLUTION PROVIDERS

Most of this book is aimed firmly at the professional procurement and supply chain audience. But we'll finish with some of the advice I gave to those on the supply side, who have to deal with procurement professionals. Actually, there is advice here on both how to write good business content and how to present at conferences that is relevant to procurement professionals, too, if they indulge in those activities.

Make the Most of That Conference Slot

Solution providers invest a lot of time and money in conferences and similar opportunities to get in front of potential clients. Spending £10,000 or even more is not unusual, and that may well get you a speaking slot as well as a corner of the exhibition room (next to the Gents and in the firing line for the freezing draught from the broken air conditioning system).

Yet time after time, over the years, we see providers using those opportunities so badly that not only do they fail to generate the leads and business that they should, they also can actually act as a negative in terms of the firm's overall image and reputation.

Talking to an experienced and very successful marketing head in our industry recently, I asked him (or was it her – let me keep some mystery here) how they would approach such opportunities. Please note, this isn't intended to be self-serving – this is a genuine view from a professional marketer.

'I've got a clear list of preferences for speakers. My number one is an independent industry expert – it might be someone from Spend Matters, Forrester or similar, or an independent ex-CPO perhaps. They tend to be trusted, and they're generally good speakers as that's part of their business. You can't control what they say totally but get them to speak on a topic that plays to your marketing proposition and that's enough to get the audience motivated and interested. You can follow up later with the specifics.'

'Number two is applicable if you are lucky enough to have a colleague who has a reputation beyond simply their role in the firm. If they are a respected industry figure, or had a life before they joined you, then that can work well in a similar way to the independent expert – although they won't be seen as quite so independent perhaps.'

'Thirdly, customers. They can be great, but you can't really control their content, you can't guarantee how good they're going to be (it's unusual to be able to get them to practise with you) so it can be a bit of a high-risk approach.'

'Finally, our own account managers, directors, and so on. Delegates just expect a sales pitch and you start with a negative perception before they've even opened their mouths.'

My personal view is that a really good customer testimonial wins every time, but which option do most firms take? Yes, you've guessed it. 45 minutes of the account director giving the standard features and benefits pitch, or even worse, the technical architect with 37 screenshots, showing in far more detail than you could possibly have imagined just how you can do supplier onboarding or approve requisitions with the new version 7.3 of their software.

People have made the effort to leave their office and come and listen. Feel honoured that they've come to spend their time with you. Be interesting. Be challenging. Be funny. Make them think. Educate them (but not about screen number 11 of the supplier onboarding process).

And there's no shame in admitting that you or your account director isn't the person to achieve that – but if you can't do so, then please get someone who can.

***

Thoughts on Dealing with CPOs

Talking to a friend over the holidays who still has the sort of large organisation Procurement Director / CPO (Chief Procurement Officer) role I held some years back, I was remembering both the delights and pressures of that type of role. Which also got me thinking about the people who had to try and sell to me.

That applies to firms selling goods and services for general organisational use – everything from IT to packaging, milk powder to legal services in my time as a practitioner – but also more specifically to those who were trying to sell me goods or services aimed at procurement directly. That included recruitment firms, software or solutions providers, consultants and the like. So, I thought I'd offer some views on how those firms and individuals might have maximised their chances of success, at least in terms of dealing with me.

Please don't think I'm being condescending here. This isn't aimed at experienced sales and account management people, who no doubt know a lot more about selling successfully to CPOs than I ever will. But maybe there will be points in here that might strike a few chords with readers and help to structure approaches to potential clients. For procurement practitioners reading this, I'd love to hear your views on how you would advise the sales community.

So, a quick look inside the CPO's head.

Please realise that we are busy. I know that is true for everyone, but just consider this. A large organisation may have perhaps 10,000 suppliers. It may be 100,000. Even if we weed out the inconsequential and occasional, there may be something like 500 to 1,000 supply-side firms to whom the CPO is an important person, within a significant customer organisation.

And that's just the current suppliers. You can probably multiply that by three or four in terms of the organisations who would *like* to be suppliers. So, don't take it personally when you find it difficult to get into my diary. There are literally thousands of people trying to do the same. Sorry, I'm not being difficult, it's just how it is. That means you need to give me a reason to see you, particularly if you're not a current supplier.

Unsolicited mail stands very little chance of getting into my hands. If I have a PA, (s)he will deal with it – if I don't, it may not even get opened or it will probably be filed in the bin immediately. Ditto unsolicited emails. Actually, a well-written personal letter (not just a junk mail circular) probably stands more chance than an email these days, as it at least it has the element of novelty.

Press releases in the main are a waste of time. I don't read them, and I'm pretty good at spotting what is purely a PR piece if it does find its way into a trade journal or other media. But industry credibility does matter and have value. If I hear positive comments about you from my CPO friends and networking compatriots, or I read a positive independent piece in Spend Matters (or other credible media outlets), that does make a difference. But note again, we don't have much time for casual reading or research, and we don't all read the same material – not even Spend Matters!

But if you have no presence outside your own website, and the odd bog-standard PR release, then it will be hard to get into my field of visibility.

If you can get through that initial barrier, then recognise that I don't have a lot of personal discretionary budget. I was once a CPO responsible for over $3 billion annual spend, and beyond my direct staff costs, I had a budget of about $300,000 a year to cover recruitment costs, training, consulting support, data, conferences, and more. I will need to develop a new business case to buy any significant software, for instance, probably even if it is on an annual licence basis.

Not only are we busy, and relatively poor, we also have short attention spans! We're not (in most cases) technologists or particularly interested in the details of your technology itself, if that's what you're selling. We do want solutions.

Now most sales training will tell you that you need to get to understand our problems and issues before you can sell to us. That's great in theory, we don't disagree. But if we give you 45 minutes, that's what we mean, and if you spend 40 minutes of that listening sympathetically while we pour out our hearts and problems to you, then you have precisely five minutes to tell us what you and your product can do. OK, we might give you another shot if we really liked the way you nodded sympathetically, but we might not, or that second bite might be in three months' time. If you're lucky.

So why not do as much of that 'establishing the need' as you can before you see me? Indeed, it is rarely sensible for your first sales meeting to be with the CPO. Start with someone at middle level in procurement – probably easier to get their interest or time, and they might even let you buy them a coffee or a glass of something after work.

Use that primarily to understand how your offering might fit with the organisation, what their needs are, what the key issues troubling them might be. Then you can compress that discovery element of the meeting with the CPO, show that you already have a pretty good understanding of the organisation and its drivers, and make sure you have time to talk about your solution.

Then, please present the product or service to us in terms of the benefits to us and how it will actually make our lives easier, better or more successful. We don't need to know all the technicalities at this stage. Sell the solution and the benefits, not the features.

I know that is really obvious, and again it is sales training school 'day one' stuff, but you'd be surprised. And if you can't get those benefits across to me in 15 minutes or so, then there's a problem. Either you're not explaining it right, or the benefits aren't really there.

But we're nice people really – so good luck!

**

But Will Anyone Read It? Writing Content for a Procurement Audience

It is ironic that just a few years after we were all predicting that the Internet, texting and Facebook would mean the end of people writing anything longer than a one-paragraph email, more people are writing more material for public consumption than ever before.

Whilst the number of professional journalists may have declined, the number of people who write blogs, content for business or personal websites, or even comment on other public websites is far greater than a few years ago. I suspect there are millions of people who now write something that (they hope) will be read by others, on a regular basis (even if they don't get paid for it).

I want to talk here specifically about the sort of material that is aimed at a professional procurement and supply chain audience. That includes blogs, papers or research reports, newsletters, news items on websites, and so on. It is very obvious that more and more firms on the supply side of the industry – software firms, consultancies, even recruitment firms – are trying to get their message across to potential and actual customers through written material of this type.

They do it for a number of valid reasons – to demonstrate 'thought leadership', directly promote their wares, develop a relationship with their customer base, or generate leads. This advice mainly applies to readers (and writers) on the supply side – although, actually, procurement practitioners could usefully follow the same tips when they're communicating internally, with stakeholders or suppliers.

So, I'm offering a few thoughts that might be useful if you find yourself in the position of writing this type of material, in part because I'm seeing some material being published that I honestly believe is having a negative effect for the firms promoting the material – it would be better to do nothing. The suggestions here are therefore around the positioning of this sort of material, and to address some common flaws, rather than a style guide. Let's consider four common mistakes.

Point 1 – Don't be overambitious

I saw a published article last week, from a specialist procurement consulting firm – 'How to buy consulting services'. I was interested to see what the author had to say, as that was the topic of the book I co-authored with Fiona Czerniawska (*Buying Professional Services: How to get value for money from consultants and other professional services providers*). We wrote 90,000 words on it, and felt we'd just about covered most – not all – of the key issues. This new piece was under 150 words. I've seen another article recently – from a software firm this time – claiming to explain IT Services procurement in about 300 words.

You just can't do it. You will either skate over the surface at the very highest level, or in reality focus on one or two individual issues or areas. And there's nothing wrong with that focus. It's why we don't write blogs on Spend Matters called 'How to do Procurement'. It is far better to focus on a manageable subject for the length of the piece you are writing, rather than suggesting you're going to cover a huge topic in a few words.

So, in the case of the professional services example, you could look at some market news, or recent trends you see as a provider in a particular sector. Or focus on an element of the overall process – for example, maybe in the professional services case, a quick analysis of the pros and cons of using fixed-price contracts (although frankly even that might be too large a subject for a 200-word blog!) But don't try and cover a huge subject in a single short article. It is rarely useful to the reader and does not generally impress anyone.

Point 2 – Be credible
You've got one of a limited number of goals when you write for a professional audience. You might be purely trying purely to entertain, although that is rare. More often, you are trying to achieve one or more of these objectives (and there is some overlap):

- *educate* – about your product or service, an aspect of procurement, a new process
- *inform* – provide information, insight or news
- *stimulate* – get people thinking, campaign on an issue, promote an idea

Most business writing – certainly in the case of blogs, articles and similar – falls into the first two categories. So, if you are trying to educate or inform, it should go without saying that what you're writing about needs to be credible. It helps if you are *personally* credible – professors can get away with writing stuff you or I couldn't – but most importantly, the content must be credible.

This is where some material can without a doubt be worse than no communication at all. I've seen articles that just made me think, 'This person doesn't know what they're talking about!' Not surprisingly, that doesn't make me want to go out and buy their products, engage them as consultants, or tell my friends about their articles.

A common problem is that senior people are busy. The task of writing the blog gets delegated therefore to someone junior who isn't a real expert, because the person who could and should write it is too busy earning fees. But the professional audience spots this a mile away. Again, I've seen a series of articles in a major procurement publication recently that I guarantee made any experienced person reading them think, 'Well, that's one firm I won't be asking for advice!' If you can't be bothered – or haven't the time – to do it well, don't do it at all.

Point 3 – Be interesting!
We are all bombarded by so many different sources of information. If you want me to spend 10 minutes – or even two minutes – reading your site, blog or article, it needs to be interesting and grab my attention, even if its underlying purpose is education / information. Consider it a privilege if anyone gives up even a few minutes of their busy day to read what you have written – that is honestly how I think about everything I write for Spend Matters. If you only write occasionally, it is even more important you get into that mindset.

And think carefully about the length and design of it. Readers will download and read a long paper if the topic and content really grab them. But they don't tend to read 5,000-word essays on the screen – and that getting more of an issue with the growth of mobile devices. I saw a good article on a website recently, based on a CPO round-table discussion, but when I scrolled down the page and saw that it went on and on and on, I admit I didn't even start reading it. If necessary, break it up into several parts.

One way to avoid being boring is to offer opinion – that's certainly a secret of success for Spend Matters and many other well-read blogs and websites. You might want to avoid the most controversial topics – nobody expects to read a polemic about immigration in the middle of an article on sourcing software. But some considered opinion in the midst of straightforward facts and information breaks up the material.

One personal bête noire is surveys. Not the idea in itself; some firms, from A.T. Kearney to State of Flux and Future Purchasing do good surveys and present interesting results. But it is when the data is played back to me without analysis or interpretation that things get truly dull.

'48% of CPOs think supply chain risk is a very important factor. 33% think it is quite important.'

SO WHAT?! What are you trying to tell me? What do you think I should do about it? What are the smartest people in procurement actually *doing* in the field of risk management? The survey results in themselves are nothing. Whatever you're writing, the basic rule is the same – if it is boring, people will stop reading.

Point 4 – Don't be condescending

Pitching the material at the right level to a professional audience is another tough one. Getting into too much detail (about new technology, for instance) and lapsing into technobabble is likely to leave many readers, even procurement professionals, behind. Many software providers still make the mistake of selling the features of the products, rather than the benefits, in their writing. (One reason for Coupa's success, I'm sure, is the clear and businesslike way they write about their products and what they can bring to users – often with a lacing of levity as well, which helps.)

But at the same time, if you're going to write an article that says, 'procurement is jolly important' and not a lot more, then readers may assume you don't know much yourself (see point 2 – 'Be Credible'.) Or, and this is just as dangerous for the writer, the reader will assume that you think they are stupid. So being seen as condescending is another danger.

That's not to say there isn't a place for pretty basic 'how to' educational material – or a beginner's guide to e-procurement (which I might read myself). But I would position it very carefully. If your newsletter is aimed at CPOs, a beginner's guide is not suitable content. If you're blogging on topics like that, then at least explain: 'This week's blog is aimed at new entrants to the profession – we thought it might be useful to describe the basics of category management.' Fine, I can now choose whether I read on or not.

Equally, if you are going to get into the innermost workings of the new e-invoicing and collaborative supplier management platform, including the intricacies of platform design and integration options, then you don't want to publish it on a news-based website or in a usually chatty blog. Understand your audience, don't be condescending, and target what you're writing about at the particular platform and who you want / might be expected to read it.

We hope this has been useful – and I would stress that I don't want to discourage anyone from writing. The more people we have adding to the body of procurement knowledge, opinion and analysis, the better. But it's worth putting a bit of effort into how you go about it, to make sure it is benefiting your organisation, and not having a negative impact.

What the Experts Say

'Peter Smith is both a procurement thought leader and an effective writer. His articles over the years have been not just useful for procurement people, but interesting for all business people.' *Bob Beveridge, FTSE 100 CFO, NED, Audit Chair and Mentor*

'Peter's articles are a great source of inspiration and industry expertise – he's highly regarded within the industry and a go-to for procurement expertise and insight.' *Sarah Childs, Group Head of Procurement, GLH Hotels*

'Peter's insightful and penetrating writing demonstrates he has been the ever-watchful guardian of good procurement for many years. His is both the voice and the conscience of our profession, particularly in the UK public service.' *Andy Davies, Head of Procurement, the Natural History Museum*

'Peter's vast experience and expertise across the whole spectrum of procurement is entertainingly captured in this collection and it comes highly recommended for all who are involved in both buying and selling.' *George Owens, CIPS European Procurement & Supply Chain Professional of the Year 2017 and Director of Procurement, Manchester Airports Group*

'I looked at Peter's articles every day if I really wanted to know what was going on in the commercial world. They became an essential read for the procurement professional, always topical and able to uniquely combine tips on best practice with breaking news, humour, gossip and even music!' *David Smith CB, CIPS Past President and Former Government Commercial Director*

'Peter Smith spent years educating and entertaining me with his blog while I was helping to build a software business aimed at those people who buy for a living. In this book, he has assembled some of his most insightful and entertaining articles. If you are looking to serve that audience of people who buy stuff, and you want to do it well, whilst seeing how procurement relates to music, corruption, technology and even Renaissance Italy, read this book.' *Garry Mansell FCIPS, former CEO of Trade Extensions Ltd*

About the Author

Peter Smith was born in Sunderland in the north-east of England and studied at St John's College, Cambridge. He fell into procurement at Mars Confectionery, decided he liked it, then worked as Procurement Director / CPO for Dun & Bradstreet Corporation (Europe), the Department of Social Security and the NatWest Group. He worked as a consultant for some years, advising government bodies such as Her Majesty's Treasury and the National Audit Office as well as many businesses, then in 2010 launched Spend Matters UK/Europe with Jason Busch (who founded Spend Matters in the US back in 2006). He was Managing Editor there for eight years, writing some 3 million words about procurement and related topics, and also worked with Public Spend Forum. He co-wrote his first book, *Buying Professional Services*, published by the Economist Books in 2010, and has lectured on the University of Birmingham MBA course, as well as speaking at many procurement events around the world and acting as an "expert witness" on procurement matters in a number of court cases. He is a Fellow and was 2003 President of the Chartered Institute of Procurement and Supply, and has served as a non-executive director for two major UK public sector organisations and a successful private sector business

Index

278

INDEX